Dr. Michael Hare's new book is a carefully craft
greatest tragedies in our churches is the massiv
Too often, there is an explosion resulting in an .
reeling with hurt, disillusionment, and even doubting or abandoning their faith. Dr. Hare
myth that all conflict is negative and helps the reader see it as an opportunity and challenge for skill-
fully designed growth. Moreover, he does not leave us with only understanding conflict, he provides us
with a model and a workbook for implementation and team building. This is an important book filled
with new hope and opportunities for transformational change. I highly recommend it!

JUDITH MCKAY
Director of Conflict Resolution Studies at Nova Southeastern University

Conflict! Few like it; many ignore it; most misunderstand it. Yet, when church leaders look to the Holy
Spirit for guidance, and engage in healthy practices, it is a golden opportunity for transformative growth.
When Church Conflict Happens shows you how to redeem conflict in your church for God's glory.

GARY L. MCINTOSH
Writer, speaker, and professor, Talbot School of Theology, Biola University

It is a pleasure to recommend Michael Hare's work *When Church Conflict Happens*. While there is much
in print about conflict, I found Michael's treatment to be a refreshing balance of comprehensive text-
book-level help and highly engaging, readable narrative. Best suited for local church leadership, you
can either use this book as a "how to" in walking through a present situation or as a proactive and amplified guide to launch an army of people trained to handle conflicts of any type. Probably most helpful
for me was a surprisingly simple mix of new vocabulary and a categorical grid that lets you make sense
of any conflict. Michael has translated his years of pastoral experience and conflict consultation into a
well-written gift to the church. Nicely done!

STEVE HIGHFILL
District Superintendent, EFCA West

In *When Church Conflict Happens*, Michael Hare provides a valuable contribution to the understanding
of conflict in churches and a biblically rooted approach to dealing with them. Michael eloquently artic-
ulates the need to identify the root causes of conflicts, provides numerous case examples, and suggests
specific skills to address them. This book is invaluable for all church leaders looking to confront conflict
constructively and to create an environment where "healthy" conflict is used for creation and growth.

JONATHAN BARTSCH
Principal, CDR Associates

For more than twenty years, Mike pastored churches that had been decimated by conflict, guiding
them through healing and restoration to growth. Seeing that most of the devastation these churches
had suffered could have been prevented inspired Mike to return to school to earn a PhD in Conflict
Analysis and Resolution with his research and dissertation focusing on church conflict.
   In this book, Mike distills the principles he has learned and practical skills he has honed through
decades of ministry as a pastor, professional mediator, and church consultant helping churches transform painful conflict into a catalyst for healing and transformation.

EDDY HALL
CEO and Senior Consultant, Living Stones Associates

Do you want to change congregational conflict into a transformative experience? Dr. Hare shows you how with systemic analysis and interventional processes. His work is anchored in Scripture and laced with real examples.

SHEROD MILLER
Author of *Working Together: Collaborative Communication Skills*
CEO, Interpersonal Communication Programs, Inc.

When Church Conflict Happens is a timely, practical guidebook for pastors and church communities seeking to wage differences constructively to achieve win-win outcomes. Dr. Mike Hare's wonderful new book points out that while conflict is functional and healthy, church leaders and their flocks need appropriate conflict-resolution tools embedded in Scripture to transform disputes into peaceful outcomes that work for the betterment of local communities. This is a must-read book for those interested in resolving conflicts constructively within religious congregations.

SEAN BYRNE
Founding director of the Peace and Conflict Studies graduate program (2005–2014), and founding director of the Arthur V. Mauro Centre for Peace and Justice (2003–2018) at the University of Manitoba

Few things break God's heart more, and cause the hosts of hell to rejoice more, than conflict among His followers. Conflict in the church is normal, inevitable, and often, necessary—but it doesn't have to end in failure. It's been said that in the Chinese language, the word "crisis" is composed of two characters, one representing *danger* and the other, *opportunity*. Conflict truly can be an opportunity for redemption, growth, and transformation. You hold in your hands a very important kingdom book. My friend Mike Hare is well-qualified to prepare church leaders with practical intervention strategies (brought to life by case stories) that enable us to anticipate, analyze, and resolve conflict, moving step-by-step through processes that result in unity and blessing. And even in those instances when a congregation is ultimately unable to prevail, the goal should still be to do the work required for the healing of relationships that allows us to honor God and finish well.

WESS STAFFORD
President Emeritus, Compassion International
Author of *Too Small to Ignore* and *Just a Minute*

Most pastors receive little or no training in conflict resolution. And yet conflict is a part of even healthy relationships and thus is part of every church. In *When Church Conflict Happens*, Michael Hare masterfully shows readers how to identify the root cause of conflict and how to respond to each type of conflict in a healthy, godly way. (That alone is worth the price of the book.) Michael then gives multiple practical examples to illustrate each type of conflict and gives the reader opportunities to practice their conflict resolution skills through those examples.

If your church is not currently in conflict, I would encourage you to praise God for that and read this book before conflict breaks out. It will give you wisdom and insight to lead and quite possibly prevent the conflict from occurring. If your church is experiencing conflict, I would encourage you to read this book to learn how to resolve the conflict and grow from it. *When Church Conflict Happens* is easy to read and is a great resource for any pastor. I'm excited to see the eternal impact God brings from this book as churches model godly resolution in the midst of conflict.

KEN COOPER
Lead Pastor, West Evangelical Free Church

WHEN CHURCH CONFLICT HAPPENS

*A Proven Process
for Resolving Unhealthy
Disagreements and
Embracing Healthy Ones*

MICHAEL HARE

MOODY PUBLISHERS

CHICAGO

Scripture quotations, unless otherwise indicated, are from the ESV® Bible (The Holy Bible, English Standard Version®), copyright 2001 by Crossway, a publishing ministry of Good News Publishers. Used by permission. All rights reserved.

Scripture quotations marked NKJV are taken from the New King James Version®. Copyright © 1982 by Thomas Nelson. Used by permission. All rights reserved.

Scripture quotations marked (NIV) are taken from the Holy Bible, New International Version®, NIV®. Copyright © 1973, 1978, 1984, 2011 by Biblica, Inc.™ Used by permission of Zondervan. All rights reserved worldwide. www.zondervan.com The "NIV" and "New International Version" are trademarks registered in the United States Patent and Trademark Office by Biblica, Inc.™

Scripture quotations marked (AMP) are from the Amplified Bible, Copyright © 2015 by The Lockman Foundation. Used by permission. www.Lockman.org.

Scripture quotations marked MSG are taken from THE MESSAGE, copyright © 1993, 1994, 1995, 1996, 2000, 2001, 2002 by Eugene H. Peterson. Used by permission of NavPress. All rights reserved. Represented by Tyndale House Publishers, Inc.

All emphasis in Scripture has been added.

Edited by Pamela J. Pugh
Interior design: Ragont Design
Cover design: Erik M. Peterson
Cover illustrations copyright © 2018 by CSA-Archive/iStock (1003562168). All rights reserved.

Library of Congress Cataloging-in-Publication Data

Names: Hare, Michael (S. Michael), author.
Title: When church conflict happens : a proven process for resolving
  unhealthy disagreements and embracing healthy ones / Michael Hare.
Description: Chicago : Moody Publishers, [2019] | Includes bibliographical
  references.
Identifiers: LCCN 2018061484 (print) | LCCN 2019001677 (ebook) | ISBN
  9780802496836 (ebook) | ISBN 9780802418371
Subjects: LCSH: Church controversies. | Church management. | Conflict
  management--Religious aspects--Christianity. | Church consultation.
Classification: LCC BV652.9 (ebook) | LCC BV652.9 .H423 2019 (print) | DDC
  254--dc23
LC record available at https://lccn.loc.gov/2018061484

Some of the accounts in this book are based on composites of actual events, but details of locations, churches, and persons have been significantly altered. Any similarities to actual events or individuals are coincidental and in no case are intended to represent any actual church interventions.

All websites listed herein are accurate at time of publication but may change in the future or cease to exist. The listing of websites and resources does not imply publisher endorsement of the site's entire contents. Groups and organizations are listed for informational purposes, and listing does not imply publisher endorsement of their activities.

We hope you enjoy this book from Moody Publishers. Our goal is to provide high-quality, thought-provoking books and products that connect truth to your real needs and challenges. For more information on other books and products written and produced from a biblical perspective, go to www.moodypublishers.com or write to:

Moody Publishers
820 N. LaSalle Boulevard
Chicago, IL 60610

1 3 5 7 9 10 8 6 4 2

Printed in the United States of America

This book is dedicated to my loving wife, Colleen, whose sacrifice and partnership have provided the foundation and inspiration for a lifetime of ministry through the wonderful family God has given us.

Contents

APPENDIXES

Foreword

Conflict often troubles us like a fly buzzing around our head. It's annoying and distracting, but does not seem to warrant an immediate response. But at other times, it comes at us like a swarm of bees, stinging from multiple directions, impossible to deflect and eventually forcing us to flee relationships out of pain, hopelessness, or fear.

This book provides an insightful, practical, and encouraging way to defend against and eventually overcome these kinds of challenges. Michael has brought years of experience as a pastor and fellow peacemaker to bear on these issues, thereby providing a valuable resource for individual Christians as well as church and ministry leaders.

Michael accurately describes many of the common causes of conflict and the lasting damage it can bring to friendships, families, businesses, and all too often, even the church, which is supposed to be a refuge of unity and peace.

The book then addresses the common mistakes most of us, including seasoned pastors, make, usually because we react to conflict out of emotion and habit rather than respond to it with thoughtful reasoning and carefully developed skills.

The discussion then moves toward hopeful and practical solutions.

Touching on a theme I've taught for many years, Michael reminds us that since all aspects of our lives are under God's loving control, every conflict is actually an opportunity to bring glory to God, to serve other people and to grow to be more like Christ.

This conviction provides strong motivation for improving our peacemaking skills. Michael supports this process in several ways.

He presents all of the key skills and principles in the context of realistic case studies. This forces us to move beyond theory and speculation and to begin wrestling through real-life issues and learning practical and powerful tools for preventing and resolving conflict.

This learning process is greatly facilitated by the many practical exercises Michael weaves into every lesson, presenting us with multiple opportunities to evaluate and apply the biblical principles set forth in this book.

These case studies and exercises enable us to look at a wide variety of conflict situations and dynamics, ranging from inner struggles, to one-on-one conflicts and differences that enflame an entire group of people. They also allow us to consider a variety of conflict styles and the way that our individual personalities and spiritual gifts can make conflict worse or better.

The Workbook section of this book is especially helpful, because it is so detailed and practical. As an engineer, lawyer, and Bible teacher, I love this kind of specific and systematic information and guidance.

I enthusiastically endorse this book and welcome it as a valuable addition to the growing stable of peacemaking resources!

KEN SANDE
Author of *The Peacemaker* and Founder of Peacemaker Ministries and Relational Wisdom 360

Introduction

All churches have conflict. Wherever there are human relationships, sooner or later, there is conflict.

The question is not if churches will have conflict but what church leaders should do about it. The good news is that conflict, as painful as it is, provides a transformational opportunity like few others—both for church leaders and for their congregations. The bad news is that not many churches seize this golden opportunity and instead allow disagreement and division to do tremendous damage. It doesn't have to be this way.

In the fellowship hall of a huge, four-story church building sat the leaders of Calvary Community Church. "This church is dying," Pastor Greg told them.

Greg Rosen had been called to a deeply divided congregation to serve as interim pastor because of his experience in helping struggling congregations. "I can help you navigate the challenges we are facing, but even if we do everything right from this point forward, at best this church has a fifty/fifty chance of survival," he told the group gathered.

Later, at home, his wife, Darci, asked, "Do you think Calvary Church will make it?"

"I don't know," Greg answered. And they agreed that it would take a miracle of grace for that to happen.

In Calvary's glory days the whole building had buzzed with six hundred worshipers, an exciting youth group, and lively children's ministries. As the neighborhood had changed over the years, attendance had steadily declined. By the time they called Pastor Greg to assess their situation, only eighty people were attending on an average Sunday. The church was failing, and all but a handful of the members admitted it.

The way most of them were handling the situation was by forming a circular firing squad and blaming one another for the church's demise. For a church with only eighty people, it was amazing how many factions the church had splintered into.

Pastor Greg had been at Calvary less than six months. At his first board meeting, the board members seated on one side of the table refused to talk with those on the other. Half of them had been glad to see the previous pastor forced out; the other half felt betrayed. Things hadn't gotten any better since.

The church was burning through the last of its funds and was using a designated gift to bring in an interim pastor as a desperate attempt to see if anything could be done to save the church. Greg suspected it was too late. While he told the leaders that their chance of survival was at best fifty/fifty even if they did everything right, he actually feared that guess was optimistic. One of Greg's strong recommendations was to bring in an outside party, in this case someone from the district level of their denomination, to provide some neutral counsel. And he assured the flock that God cared more than anyone else for this small congregation.

Two days after that meeting, Pastor Greg received a call from the board chair. "I understand what you told us in our last meeting," he said. "I've met with the elders again, and we realize that even if we try to work through our differences and do everything you recommend, we may not survive. But we have decided to work together—the elders and members in other key positions—and follow your leadership. We agree about calling in someone from the denomination. We hope that by God's grace we can turn our church around, but if we can't, we don't want things to end with all these broken relationships. We want our relationships to be healed and to be a good testimony, whether the church survives or not. If we're going to die, we want to finish well."

The Opportunities
That Conflict Can Bring

And so the partnership between these leaders and their new pastor began in earnest. It took months for those willing to work through several significant issues to see results, but after a time, most of the divisions within the church had been healed. And the vast majority of the congregation had united around a shared vision. Those few naysayers who didn't support the church's new direction had lost their influence. The church's health had improved dramatically, and the atmosphere of gloom and doom eventually gave way to one of excitement and hope.

Calvary Community Church turned its crisis into an opportunity. There was no magic bullet. But over a couple of years of energetic, creative work and the leadership looking to the Holy Spirit for guidance, this congregation experienced an amazing transformation.

Avoid ignoring conflict

Calvary Church almost waited too long. When I asked a church conflict consultant with over thirty years of experience, "What is the greatest challenge you face in your work with churches?" he answered, "I get called into a church three days after it burns down." Why do so many church leaders wait so long?

One common reason is the "all conflict is bad" mentality. When someone questions a policy or a decision, these leaders' instinct is to silence those who are "making waves."

Another reason is that dealing with conflict involves risk. If we confront someone about their bad behavior, we risk rejection. If that person resists our feedback, it is painful for both of us.

Yet another reason church leaders avoid conflict is that they just don't know what to do.

Do not resist help

At Crossroads Church, all these factors were at work. Pastor Jerry Jordan was a gifted and passionate teacher, and he was appreciated for his kindness and compassion. Because of his gift of compassion, he was highly attuned to people and put great value on protecting their feelings.

One way this tendency expressed itself was that when gifted staff and laypeople in the church would point out areas that needed improvement, Jerry perceived their suggestions as "rocking the boat." Because he didn't want anyone's feelings to get hurt, he usually dismissed the concerns that were raised.

Over the years, most of the strategic leaders at Crossroads realized that their voices were never going to be heard, so they moved to other churches where they had more opportunities to use their gifts. Leadership teams were gradually filled with people who had similar personalities to Pastor Jerry, resulting in this conflict-avoidance attitude taking root in the culture of the church. People had such high respect for their pastor that conflict seldom surfaced, but it was always still there, just below the surface.

By the time Pastor Jerry retired, all the tension that had been suppressed spewed out. Over the next few months, as things turned ugly, 40 percent of the congregation left. The only thing that had kept the volcano from erupting earlier was deference to their beloved pastor. When Pastor Jerry heard what was happening to the church that he had poured himself into for fifteen years, he was heartsick.

Navigate conflict with confidence

The good news is that disasters like Calvary Community and Crossroads Church endured can be avoided. Church leaders can create an environment where healthy conflict is nurtured (yes, healthy conflict is essential to maximum creativity) and where unhealthy conflict becomes an opportunity for growth. We can learn how to have difficult conversations in ways that make positive outcomes more likely. We can learn to see beneath the presenting issues to the root causes of conflict, and develop practical skills for growing a healthier church culture.

As church leaders, we don't have the luxury of viewing conflict as an intrusion into our work. Conflict is normal; it is part of everyday life. Managing conflict creatively to bring greater health and effectiveness to the church is one of the core responsibilities of church leaders.

The Approach This Book Will Take

This book is designed to help the reader gain a clear recognition of the problems that can occur when trying to resolve church conflict. Included are some common mistakes made by church leaders (Section One) and information on how to create a functional model for analyzing and resolving these conflicts—in a biblical and healthy manner (Section Two). Finally, Section Three offers some practical exercises and tools to help church leaders evaluate and implement the model. (Numerous examples and case studies are provided, illustrating both the problems and their solutions, and step-by-step guidance is given in how to implement the model.) The chapters and examples build on one another and are developed in such a way as to reveal the connections between theory and practice. This approach does require the reader to follow along closely with the process, chapter by chapter, in order to fully benefit from this model.

Important Disclaimer

Although many of the stories used in this book as examples are based on actual events, they have been altered to avoid revealing any individual or church identities. In most cases, these stories are composites of several cases with significant changes made to protect identities of both individuals and churches. In the remainder of examples, they are fictionalized accounts based on my experiences that represent common conflict scenarios that could happen in most congregations over time. Any similarities to actual churches or events are coincidental and not intended to correlate to any actual individual church interventions.

You don't need to dread conflict. You can learn to make the most of the opportunities it offers to transform your church for good.

SECTION ONE

THE
PROBLEM

Chapter 1

Why Your Church Needs Conflict

Consider it nothing but joy, my brothers and sisters, whenever you fall into various trials. Be assured that the testing of your faith [through experience] produces endurance [leading to spiritual maturity, and inner peace]. And let endurance have its perfect result and do a thorough work, so that you may be perfect and completely developed [in your faith], lacking in nothing.
—James 1:2–4 AMP

When church leaders and members are willing to honestly accept, openly confess, and intentionally address the underlying causes of church conflict, God will repair and restore the church.[1]
—Jim Van Yperen

"These kids need this money!" Jane's voice revealed her resolve.

Everyone at the table watched for what would happen next. Jane represented a growing youth ministry and found herself in the middle of an emotionally charged discussion about how to use a large sum recently donated to the church.

"We really need to provide summer activities for this flood of new kids. God brought them to us, and we can't afford to miss this opportunity. Our team has located a youth camp for sale that would be perfect. I say we act on this before it is too late."

"Not so fast," Brad, the trustee board chair, replied. "All those kids came with parents too!" He added, "Our sanctuary is bursting at the seams, and I say we use this gift to make room in the sanctuary for these new families—they're the ones who will be paying for the future of our ministry."

Wes, the adult ministry pastor, agreed. "Our classroom space is already stretched to the max, and unless we do something soon, this constraint alone will stop our growth. We need a master building plan that serves all our ministries equally."

The debate continued with strong opinions and passionate pleas. Pros and cons were vigorously expressed around the table. As a guest observer—invited because of my experience in facilitating group problem-solving—my adrenaline was pumping and my mind was racing, and I wondered when it was all going to come off the rails. I'd been in too many meetings like this one, where tempers explode and relationships are irreparably damaged. But what happened next caught me completely off guard. After an hour of lively discussion, the elder leading the meeting indicated that time was up and that this debate would need to continue later.

Right when I thought people might stomp out of the room, something very different had happened. Jane sought out Brad and said, "Wow, you put up a pretty tough argument. Good job!"

Brad responded, "I haven't seen you this serious in a long time. That camp sounds great; I'm sure we can get to the right decision with God's help. We are going to need to minister to those kids and their parents too. I really appreciate your dedication to our youth!"

"Give my love to Denise, Brad, and thank the other trustees for me. You guys are doing an amazing job keeping our church looking beautiful and welcoming for visitors every weekend," Jane said, smiling as she turned to head out the door.

This was the first time I had encountered church leaders who were able to fully debate emotional issues without becoming defensive or taking things personally. In the end, they managed to meet both sets of needs with the money that was available. Rather than build a new multimillion-dollar sanctuary, they worked with a consulting team to design some building and programming modifications that allowed the church to double weekend attendance while using existing facilities. They were able to use another piece of property that the church already owned for a family and youth campground for summer ministry. And, as for these leaders' relationships, they are stronger than ever!

Three Facets of Church Conflict

Church conflict is too often viewed from a negative perspective, which is too simplistic. The examples that follow illustrate three different categories of conflict: (1) unhealthy conflict, (2) benign conflict, and (3) healthy conflict.

Before attempting to resolve the church issues we face, two helpful questions need to be asked: What is at the root of the disagreement? And, How are the people responding to one another while trying to solve their problems?

Although it is true that all conflict can become unhealthy, it doesn't have to go that way. Depending on the underlying issues and how people respond, conflict can actually become a healthy platform for problem-solving and spiritual growth. Getting to the underlying factors—the root causes—provides important insights into how to do this. We will be exploring exactly how this process works.

Unhealthy conflict often goes unrecognized until interpersonal disputes and church factions begin to develop. *Benign conflict* pertains to those church disagreements that occur because of organizational deficits and oversights that are unintentional. *Healthy conflict* refers to disagreements that are recognized, acknowledged, and responded to in a biblically constructive manner.

The following cases show you how to recognize the differences between these types of conflict and how to inform leaders to both acknowledge and respond to these events in helpful ways.

Unhealthy conflict

EASTERN VALLEY CHURCH:
THE CASE OF THE UNWISE LEADERS

"How quickly can we schedule to have you come and help us?"

Jason Robinson had been pastor of Eastern Valley Church for less than ten months. The church, located in a small East Coast town, had a long and fruitful history. Until recently, its reputation was one of stability and community service as well as offering strong evangelism and mission outreaches. Pastor Robinson phoned a facilitator from the denomination for assistance, but was anxious and didn't offer much detail while answering the preliminary questions the facilitator asked. (Denominations differ greatly in the resources they can provide to help congregations in conflict. Some are great, but others may lack knowledge and skill and may even make things worse. Researching the historical effectiveness of such resources, along with evaluating outside conflict resolution specialists, is recommended before extending invitations for outside assistance.)

Arriving on a Thursday afternoon, the facilitator met with the pastor to discuss his concerns. Jason began by outlining his clear vision for the church. However, he quickly digressed into an angry diatribe aimed at what he perceived as resistance to his leadership. In fact, several long-tenured families had recently left and were attending other churches.

"I know what this church needs," Jason insisted. "Why won't anyone listen to me?"

What this denominational official learned from interviewing members of the congregation was a disturbing picture of a very sick church. Churches can become unhealthy over time for many reasons. In this case, the presenting issues were vague in nature and revealed scattered symptoms of disunity, personal hurt, and widespread distrust. Deeper inspection uncovered an ugly list of root causes related to:

- A new, inexperienced pastor who demonstrated immaturity, impatience, a lack of integrity, and a short temper.
- Leaders who were less than honest with him and with one another. Most of the people who had recently departed were, evidently, the more spiritually mature leaders and members of the congregation. They were exhausted from trying to help their new pastor turn the church around. Having failed, they gave up.
- The small group of newly appointed leaders, most of whom were new to the church, exhibited shortcomings similar to their pastor.

Eastern Valley Church was not beyond help. These conflicts could have provided opportunities to reveal needed changes that could lead to redemptive solutions. If the leaders humbled themselves and yielded to godly counsel, their best days could yet be ahead. But unfortunately, they did not. An unhealthy culture had developed and contributed to a downward spiral until the ministry failed and the church closed. The problems these leaders faced are not uncommon. What made this conflict unhealthy was the actions that were taken (or not taken) to address their problems.

In the pages ahead, we will demonstrate how conflict can serve to deepen discipleship and transform leaders.

MAIN STREET CHURCH:
THE CASE OF THE MISSED OPPORTUNITY

"This is our church, and no one is going to take it away from us!" Carl said, almost shouting. The other elders in the room nodded in agreement. "Our church has been here for over fifty years; we were here first, and we're not leaving. But, Pastor, if we do what you're suggesting, we *are* going to lose our church!" Carl's voice was quivering now, and everyone else sat in sober silence.

"But if we keep doing the same things that we've been doing, we're going to lose our church anyway," Pastor Sam said softly.

The pastor had suggested making changes to their outreach strategies—to reach a growing ethnic population in the neighborhood. This congregation was in decline and, while most of the churches in this part of town had long ago relocated to the growing edges of the city, Main Street Church had decided to stay. The building was paid for, but the congregation was aging rapidly. Sam had been pastor there for less than a year.

"Do you want to wait until the congregation is no longer able to maintain the expenses and we're forced to sell to whoever is willing to buy?" Sam asked. "This has happened to other churches that had been unwilling to change," he added.

Earlier in the meeting the elders had been enthusiastic about the new ideas for effective evangelism, with the goal of reaching the large number of minority families now occupying the surrounding community. But then the elder board chair suddenly seemed to realize some of the implications for this middle-class Caucasian congregation.

The conflict that followed revealed some unhealthy attitudes and perspectives about the mission of the church. This church had been vibrant fifteen years before. But, as often happens in cities, the neighborhood changed. High unemployment and shifting demographics were evident.

Most evangelical churches in the area had relocated to the outskirts of the metropolitan area to attract younger families. Some churches that stayed did so for the right reasons: to reach the many families moving in who needed loving congregations to welcome them. But Main Street was not one of them. Instead, the leaders fought to keep things "the way they were," and the result was to suffer the fate of an aging and dying congregation. Finally, desperate to survive, they changed pastors. And even then, it quickly became clear that it was for the wrong reasons. Suddenly, it seemed, they faced very difficult choices. Eventually, these leaders made the right decisions, but not before much conflict and loss came as a result.

Benign conflict

NORTHEAST COMMUNITY CHURCH:
THE CASE OF THE PAPER CALENDAR

Steve sat in his church office, reflecting on his last meeting. *Something else has to be going on here! This is the third time I've had to conduct a mediation session with the same leaders. And one person has been involved in all three conflicts! Maybe he is having trouble at home or work . . . but three times?*

The first disagreement was over room assignments. The next was about office supplies. And now it was about volunteers . . . Steve wondered what was next.

Each mediation session seemed to be successful at the time, with apologies exchanged and parties agreeing to reconcile. So why the repeated incidents?

No question the church was having growing pains. After a major split, the attendance had dropped from 500 to 150 on an average Sunday. Then the church once again reached the 200 mark, and a second service was added. In that first week the attendance jumped from 200 to 300, and the church never looked back.

Northeast Community Church had been operating in the "family style" of governance. Everyone knew everyone else. Formal infrastructure was rarely needed. For example, the church calendar was literally a paper desk calendar in the office, used to reserve rooms for ministry events. People were invited to pencil in their reservations week to week. But because some of the church's core ministries were so well established, those particular events were not written on the calendar—"because everyone knows not to schedule that room at that day and time."

As the church continued to grow, additional ministries formed, and the new leaders were unaware of these unwritten rules. Rooms were now being scheduled by more than one group at a time. Although these leaders were being directed to the write-in church calendar, conflicts occurred regularly because of unclear communication. On paper, an area looked available to meet in, but in practice it was not! Hence conflict. Other informal practices yielded similar results.

These conflicts had root causes that were not intentional or personal. They were the result of organizational deficits that could be corrected only through organizational changes. (We will be referring to these types of deficits as *structural* root causes.) Once the needed changes were made at Northeast, the conflicts virtually disappeared overnight.

The interpersonal disputes that were recurring were merely *presenting issues* or symptoms of the root causes that were less visible but still critical to understanding and resolving the conflicts. They are referred to here as *benign* because they do not represent *intentional, malicious,* or *sinful* acts. Rather, they are unintentional oversights due to the inexperience or ignorance of the people involved. And although it is true that sinful responses often follow such incidents, these reactions are secondary to the underlying causes that are organizational in nature. Reconciling the individual relationships is important but insufficient to correct the underlying issues.

Park Hill Missionary Church:
The Case of the Leaders Who Knew Too Little

"Let's keep praying. I know it's late and we have been here a long time, but this is just too good to miss!" Tony pleaded. The elder board and pastors were enjoying prayer times together like never before. The new focus on reaching the lost in the 10/40 Window had this leadership team more excited than ever before.[2] Tony found no opposition to his plea, and they prayed past the usual allotted time. This deep sense of unity and tremendous satisfaction was getting better and better!

It had not always been this way at Park Hill. After a brief period of division and conflict on the board a year before, this spiritual renewal was refreshing indeed. The fellowship and prayer was having a positive impact on the entire leadership team. Stirring messages from several visiting missionaries only added to their passion!

However, not everyone in the church was happy about these new outreach priorities. The people were growing concerned about decisions made regarding spending and leadership, and some of these concerns got back to those in charge.

"The board is having long meetings into the night, and many of us wonder why all the secrecy," one trustee said.

"The preaching has changed too. It's a diet of missions and evangelism every week now," complained a longtime church member.

How could the climate among leaders be so different from that in the congregation? The more people talked, the more discontent they became, and the disgruntled feelings were affecting a good number of people in the church.

The chasm between these excited leaders and their worried flock was not because of any intentional or malevolent actions by the leadership team but was instead because of a failure on their part to recognize how important good communication and collaborative decision-making is to developing ownership and unity in congregations.

In the chapters ahead, we will demonstrate how to recognize the symptoms of structural conflict and provide the tools needed to address them.

Healthy conflict

The Case of Mistaken Identity

"Pastor Bob, we need you to say something!" one of the elders said anxiously.

What started out as a transparent and friendly conversation among church leaders had become painfully awkward. And yet moments earlier, there had been amazing signs of unity and loyalty, and a surprising level of trust and camaraderie, between the leaders in this small-town Southern church.

In the months leading up to this meeting, the congregation has shown signs of unrest, and serious accusations had been made against these leaders. David Smith, a pastor from a neighboring community, had encouraged these elders to carefully investigate the list of complaints, many of them against the senior pastor. David stopped by this Sunday afternoon to observe their meeting.

As each elder reported on his assignment, the atmosphere in the room grew heavier by the minute. Although many of the accusations were unfounded and eventually dismissed, several were serious.

Pastor Bob sat in silence, making no eye contact with his leaders. A response was needed, but none was forthcoming. After what seemed like an eternity, the elders reluctantly closed the meeting.

The visiting pastor was stunned. He thought, *I've never witnessed such a failure to lead at such a critical moment.* As David got up to leave, Bob asked him to come over for dinner. They drove to Bob's house in silence. The meeting's end was so confounding that David wasn't sure how to reengage Bob in conversation.

As they sat down in the living room, Bob said, "Thank you for coming over. I think God knows that I need a friend right now; I couldn't talk about this before." He went on to describe how devastated he was to hear these accusations from his parishioners. He spoke slowly. "I'm so hurt that I don't even know what to say."

David waited and listened and soon began to realize just how deeply this man was wounded. Clearly it had taken Bob some time to process what he had heard. David thought, *I misread Bob's silence as an admission of guilt.*

Bob then unequivocally stated that the most serious accusations made against him were false. David prayed silently, *Thank You, God, for this opportunity to talk.* David subsequently was able to encourage Bob, assuring him of his continuing friendship and support.

What followed was a series of events that illustrate just how important healthy conflict can be in the life of a church. Because of a history of conflict avoidance, minor offenses and misunderstandings had festered and undermined relationships. For years, unhealthy responses to disagreement had created a toxic environment. It was clear that Bob's humility and integrity were changing the culture and uniting the hearts of his elders.

The next Sunday, Pastor Bob humbly stood before his congregation and asked forgiveness for those things for which he did feel responsible. This act set the tone for the entire congregation, and a spirit of contrition, repentance, and reconciliation followed. Those who had been untruthful and sinful in their actions and words toward the church leaders either repented, left the church, or lost all credibility. The church began to heal, and God blessed it spiritually and numerically. Now, a number of years later, disagreements are viewed as an opportunity to dig deeper. Conflict is no longer avoided but confronted biblically and redemptively.

Greenwood Bible Chapel:
The Case of a Divided Search Committee

"We've had an interim pastor long enough; it's time to call a new senior pastor!" Erica said.

The six members of the search committee were clearly

frustrated. Their last two meetings had ended in a deadlock. Half of the members felt that the church was losing valuable time. The other half felt as though more work was needed with the interim pastor before interviewing candidates. The founding pastor had retired three months previously after twenty years of successful ministry.

"We need Skip's help," said the committee chair.

Skip Baylor's service as an interim pastor was proving to be a big help during the transition. He preached each week and also met with ministry leaders to help them maintain focus and momentum. Skip was invited by the committee to their next meeting. After hearing their plight, he suggested another meeting the following Sunday afternoon. He explained that he would pose as a mock pastoral candidate and asked the committee to interview him as they would an actual candidate. Skip made a list of likely questions a prospective pastor might ask regarding the church's vision, mission, leadership, future plans, church values, philosophy of ministry, living arrangements, expectations of the pastor's family, and so on.

For more than an hour, the committee struggled to answer these questions in a satisfactory manner. At the end of the exercise, the chair called for a vote. The search team voted unanimously to work together to clarify the church's position on important issues before moving forward in the process.

Choosing to ask for help and working together likely avoided a church split. Skip's work with this congregation for another year resulted in clearly articulated ministry values and a successful pastoral search. The conflict served as a platform for asking important questions, and the leaders seized this opportunity to engage in healthy dialogue.

It is important for church leaders to recognize the differences and symptoms between healthy and unhealthy conflict. Helpful responses depend on gaining a good understanding of the conflict and conducting an accurate analysis of a number of factors. Unfortunately, all too often, any conflict is viewed through a single lens. In the next chapter, we will look at some common mistakes church leaders often make. Then, moving forward, we will set a course on how to avoid these mistakes and make the kind of decisions that can potentially transform your church!

Chapter 2

Three Common Approaches to Conflict and Why They Fall Short

If possible, so far as it depends on you, live peaceably with all.
—Romans 12:18

Reprove a wise man, and he will love you.
—Proverbs 9:8

"I just hate conflict! I'll do anything I can to avoid it," Lindsey said emphatically. "I avoid people who I think might disagree or argue with me. I steer clear of meetings where I know there will be trouble. I even stay away from church for weeks at a time when something controversial or contentious is going on." She added, "I'd rather get a root canal than deal with any kind of conflict."

Lindsey is not alone. Conflict avoidance is a primary strategy for many people, especially in the church. "The world is full of conflict. Church should be a place of peace and tranquility" is a common refrain. Conflict avoidance can manifest in a number of ways. The following categories are just a few of the ineffective strategies often used to avoid acknowledging and fully engaging conflict in a healthy manner. Although avoiding conflict is sometimes the best strategy (this will be discussed later in the book), more often than not it only postpones the inevitable and usually makes things worse.

Regarding Conflict Negatively

CHRIST'S CHURCH: PEACE AT ANY PRICE

"I've brought my concerns to the leadership board, and they have not even acknowledged my communication," Grady said.

"Did you share your concerns with the pastor?" Kent asked. Kent chaired the Healthy Community Team,[3] which had been formed at the suggestion of a mediator to help the congregation with problem-solving.

"I sent all my notes and emails directly to the pastor. I just assumed he would take them to the board."

In the next meeting with the elder board chair, Kent asked about these voiced concerns. The board chair replied, "I've never even heard about these concerns before. As far as I know, none of the elders have."

Pastor Ed Jenkins had been serving as the senior pastor of Christ's Church for just over twenty-two years. Kent scheduled a meeting and asked him if he was aware of Grady's concerns. "Oh, yes," he answered, "but I have never responded because I knew that it would just stir up the church."

"Did you take these matters to your elders as Grady asked you to do?" Kent asked.

"No. Again, I don't want to start conflict and division with our leaders or with the congregation," the pastor replied.

Many church leaders have expressed similar attitudes. We refer to this form of conflict avoidance as "peace at any price." In their minds, conflict is the worst possible of all conditions. For some, it is because of the way they are wired emotionally. For others, it is how they were raised—by parents who never let their children see their conflicts. For still others, it is shaped by their interpretation of Scripture, believing that all conflict is sinful. They either feel as though they shouldn't be having conflict because they are Christians or that it would be sinful to allow or participate in any kind of disagreement, especially in the church. And often, as in the case of Pastor Jenkins, it takes the form of conflict avoidance at all costs. Whatever the reason, conflict avoidance or constant accommodation is seldom helpful.

GRACE COMMUNITY: FIREFIGHTER APPROACH

"I'm worn out; I don't think that I can do this anymore," Pastor Sean said to his wife, Virginia. His despondence was evident. "It seems like no sooner do I solve one problem than another one pops up. I've been out every night this week putting out fires!" Virginia didn't answer.

Sean's approach to conflict resolution was to view every hint of disagreement as a fire that must be extinguished as quickly and as quietly as possible. Each time one of his parishioners or leaders smelled smoke of any kind, he rushed in to help put out the fire before it could spread. Sometimes it was a committee locked in disagreement. At other times, a conflict involved parishioners who needed help mediating family disputes. And then there was the church staff! It seemed that every week another challenging point of contention cropped up.

Pastor Sean had been operating this way for years. The fires never seemed to end, no matter how much time he devoted to putting them out. However, his approach to conflict resolution was to minimize and to accommodate, never to fully engage.

SPRINGS CHAPEL: "SPIRITUAL PROBLEM" APPROACH

"I believe that I'm under spiritual attack and that our church has been targeted by Satan. We are victims of malicious spiritual warfare," Pastor Colin O'Dell asserted.

Factions had developed in Springs Chapel and people in the congregation were actively building coalitions.

Members of the congregation had conflicting views of the senior pastor's performance. Some had a strong sense of loyalty and admiration for his courageous and bold leadership and believed he was being unfairly targeted. Others tearfully recounted experiences of being verbally attacked by the pastor in private, or even publicly in the church lobby on a Sunday morning. Some even said that the pastor had called them out from the pulpit.

What was Pastor O'Dell's response? "I am the senior pastor. I know better what this church needs than the board ever will. When someone is an instrument of the devil, you need to call them out for everyone to hear. Satan is just using them as an instrument of division to split our church and destroy me!"

Instead of explaining or providing evidence that accusations were false, this pastor seemed to equate every issue with a spiritual problem or with spiritual forces. He had been known to say to other pastors in the community, "Many in our congregation are being influenced by demonic spirits determined to undermine the Lord's anointed."

No doubt, the devil is real! And, certainly, he and his emissaries are always seeking to undermine the work of God. Someone has said, "If the devil's not in it, God probably isn't either!" So please don't misunderstand—naming this category of conflict is not meant to minimize the influence of Satan or the reality of spiritual warfare. However, to attribute every type of conflict directly to Satan is to oversimplify a complex subject. And, by doing so, church leaders can miss a great opportunity to better understand many indirect tools of the evil one that become significant keys to resolving most disputes. Pastor O'Dell, consciously or unconsciously, is simply using a different strategy to avoid healthy evaluation and biblical steps to problem-solving and reconciliation.

The Common Denominator

What do all these approaches have in common? They all view conflict negatively and fail to see the opportunities that conflict presents. They fail to seek deeper causes and react only to symptoms (presenting issues). In chapter 3, we explore a better path.

SECTION TWO

THE MODEL

Chapter 3

Demystifying Church Conflict

He who answers a matter before
he hears it, it is folly and shame to him.
—Proverbs 18:13 NKJV

If the time has not been spent to analyze what a conflict is truly
about, then negotiation may be rushed and counterproductive,
serving to exacerbate and deepen hostilities.[4]
—Jay Rothman

"You're fired! Get out of my office."

Curtis stood for a moment, stunned. As the church's youth pastor, Curtis thought that he and the senior pastor were simply discussing the best way to move the youth ministry forward. True, some parents were complaining, but nothing seemed all that serious or unusual. Youth ministry always seemed to be a tightrope walk. Pastor Les Loniger muttered something about "the last straw."

"And now I'm fired?" Curtis said out loud. He thought, *How can this be happening? We have poured our lives into this church for over ten years.* Curtis reflected on how he and his wife, Trish, had influenced the lives of so many kids who were now spiritually healthy and thriving, some in college and others they had worked with now fully in the adult world. And today, in one short moment, it's all over? Unbelievable—it's just not right! "How can you do this to me?" Curtis's voice shook as he felt a flush of anger fill his face.

After regaining some composure, Curtis half pleaded in a softer tone, "But Pastor, let's just—"

Pastor Loniger cut him off, saying, "There is nothing left to talk about. I want you out of your office before the weekend. Conversation over!"

Pastor Les and Curtis had navigated many difficult discussions in the past, most of which seemed more significant than this one, at least to Curtis.

"So, one of the parents didn't like the fact that every kid didn't have his permission slip signed for the last outing . . . Who could object to a PG-rated movie?!" Curtis reasoned under his breath. "So why are you doing this now? Why all this trouble about such a small issue?" Curtis asked the pastor.

But there was no reply. Pastor Loniger didn't even look up, but Curtis could see that the pastor's face was red. The youth pastor turned, left Les's office, and walked down the hall to his own.

Wow, I sure didn't see this one coming, he thought as he sat in his office, head still spinning, remembering several incidents over the past few months. Now in agony, Curtis's mind was racing. "In most of those cases, I made phone calls to parents. Things were worked out, weren't they?" he thought out loud, trying to regain his balance. *Could the permission slip issue really be all that is behind this inexplicable episode?* Curtis certainly didn't know, but now it seemed too late to do anything about it. Curtis and Trish were finished at White Sands Bible Church, and nothing they were going to do or say was going to change that.

Conflict Dynamics

Presenting issues

In many difficult situations, the most visible problems or presenting issues are not the real causes at the heart of the conflict.

That is why we often find ourselves baffled when people seem to be overreacting. A disproportionate gap between what happened in a particular incident and how some people are responding is a clue to deeper issues.

A parent called and reported that Pastor Curtis was not making sure students had turned in signed permission slips for a youth outing. The next day, the senior pastor, Les Loniger, fired his youth pastor of ten years, without even the appearance of due process. Pastor Loniger feels justified and Curtis feels betrayed. Unfortunately, even though a few of the students' parents are going to be gratified by this action, much of the congregation is about to explode emotionally, bringing the church to the precipice of their worst nightmare. Not only do these kids love Curtis and Trish, but so do most of the people in the church.

Because parents whose children are youth-group age are also both staff and lay leaders scattered through every ministry in the church, the divisions developing within and between groups are emerging like sleeper cells about to ignite and affect everyone and everything. It is no longer just about policies and procedures; it is about personal relationships, staff loyalty, integrity, decision-making processes, constitutional authority, and personnel matters. And as everyone is about to discover, many are convinced that it is also about biblical principles.

How did things go so terribly wrong?

Digging deeper

Organizational conflicts are often complex. Whether between individuals, ethnic groups, or nations, complex conflicts have significant histories, contexts, and perspectives to consider. A number of factors can influence both the nature of the conflicts and what is going to be needed to resolve them. To rush to a solution before a conflict is well understood almost always makes things worse.

Yet that is exactly what we as church leaders often do. At White Sands, good solutions were found over time but not before considerable damage had been done to people and relationships. The entire church suffered greatly.

Think of the last time you were embroiled in a highly emotional conflict. If you are like me and 99.9 percent of the world's population, your adrenaline began to flow, your vision narrowed, your heart began to pound, your voice got louder, and before you knew it, well, regrettable things happened. God wired us to respond defensively when we feel threatened. This very natural response is for our survival. Threatening circumstances trigger a physiological response. It therefore takes intentional and practiced behaviors to overcome these instincts and to respond differently.

Sometimes a physiological response is exactly what's needed. If we wake up in the night to the smell of smoke, our natural reflexes can serve us well. If we also respond this way when our ego is threatened or our pride is wounded, our instincts can override our thinking. Our *natural* reflexes go on automatic at times when it would be better if we had practiced a *supernatural* response enabled by the Holy Spirit. The problem is that our natural responses often feel so right in the moment that we rush in where angels fear to tread. Fortunately, God in His grace has provided a way of escape from giving in to temptation (1 Cor. 10:13).

So what has all this to do with conflict resolution? Quite a lot, actually. If we are successful at resisting the temptation to follow our "fight or flight" brain-stem response and instead allow our higher brain to make us pause long enough to respond more thoughtfully, we can often move from the presenting issue to discern what is beneath the surface. These culprits are usually not too hard to find if we know where to look. I call them "root causes." The more you practice doing this, the better you will get at recognizing and responding in healthier ways. How important is it to discover the root cause of a problem? Well, how important is it to uncover the underlying cause if you are experiencing chest pain?

Shifting gears

Think of a time when your lower brain was fully engaged for battle. I like to call it "the fog of war," and there's a reason for that. When we operate out of instinct, most of the blood supply moves away from the higher brain, the thinking part, to the reactive lower brain. When this happens, we can no longer conduct any significant evaluation or analysis; we can only react to protect whatever feels threatened. If we face immediate physical danger, this response can save our lives or the lives of others. In other situations, though, our response will not be a *thinking* one. The trick is to understand what is happening before it is too late.

Taking a mental step back and shifting gears—so to speak— can keep the blood flowing in the right direction. This takes self-discipline and self-control. Proverbs 25:28 says, "Whoever has no rule over his own spirit is like a city broken down, without walls" (NKJV). When we are stressed, we can easily react out of the flesh. Responding from our new, spiritual nature does not happen automatically. It can happen only when we intentionally submit ourselves to God's Spirit. This is accomplished through the hard work of spiritual discipline.

I recently attended training in critical incident and stress management. The instructor related a case in which the FBI requested his help on a shooting involving one of their agents. The officer was cornered by a couple of bad guys and engaged in a gun battle. When the agent ran out of ammunition, he emptied the brass cartridges on the ground and then picked them up and put them in his pocket before beginning to reload.

In the meantime, one of the assailants shot the agent. The FBI wanted the instructor, a psychologist, to help them avoid this type of problem in the future. This consultant asked the agency how they were training their personnel with firearms. They explained that on a firing range, agents were expected to "police their own brass." In other words, to pick up the shell casings each time they fired so many rounds. The psychologist concluded that the wounded agent was just performing as he was trained to do. When people are in stressful situations, the lower brain defaults to reflexive behavior and in this case to trained behavior. The agent wasn't thinking; he was just doing. As I listened to this story, my thoughts immediately turned to the Christian life. If we have not adequately trained ourselves to respond spiritually in crisis, we will default to the old nature. No wonder conflict brings out the worst in people!

Conflict level dynamics

In conflict, we need to *think* before we act. However, since threatening or stressful circumstances move us rapidly to natural reflexes, we need to practice godly responses before they are actually needed. In other words, our spiritual thinking needs to lead us to training in godliness *before* the problem arises. Our old sinful habits need to be replaced with new habits, godly habits. Good preparation requires good understanding and analysis. Sorting things out is hard when we are stressed, but picturing different levels or spheres of potential root causes can be helpful. The terms "levels of conflict" or "conflict levels" have been used in different ways in conflict resolution literature. Some authors are referring to graduated levels of "escalation" in conflict.[5] Others use a wide range of emotional and categorical topics to compare variables in conflict (roles, responses, types, and so on). Use of this term here refers to "locations" or "domains" of conflict.[6]

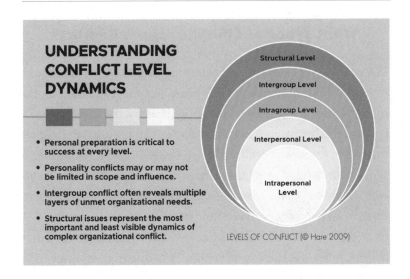

UNDERSTANDING CONFLICT LEVEL DYNAMICS

- Personal preparation is critical to success at every level.
- Personality conflicts may or may not be limited in scope and influence.
- Intergroup conflict often reveals multiple layers of unmet organizational needs.
- Structural issues represent the most important and least visible dynamics of complex organizational conflict.

Structural Level
Intergroup Level
Intragroup Level
Interpersonal Level
Intrapersonal Level

LEVELS OF CONFLICT (© Hare 2009)

The simplest place to start is in the smallest circle in the diagram: *Intrapersonal* dynamics. This circle represents the part of the conflict that resides inside of us. It includes our reflexes, our emotions, our thoughts, and, most importantly, our spiritual will. Moving outward, the next level is the *Interpersonal* sphere. This refers to the relational dynamics in a conflict involving our interactions with other people. So limiting our considerations to just a few individuals (two to five people) allows us to distinguish it from the next two levels, which consider *group dynamics* in conflict: *Intragroup* and *Intergroup*. They cover conflict both within and between groups. The last one is the *Structural* level of conflict.

This diagram serves as a "map" on which we can plot different aspects of the conflict, helping us to engage the thinking part of our brain (directing us away from a more visceral response) and informing us which next steps could be most strategic in problem-solving.

What Types of Churches Have Conflict?

The conflict between Les and Curtis described earlier is just one example of how a church conflict can begin small and then mushroom. Although it usually is best to catch such a situation early and prevent escalation, even late intervention can be successful and redemptive. At the end of this chapter, you will have an opportunity to try your hand at using these tools to analyze and develop intervention strategies for Les and Curtis's predicament. But before we do that, let's consider an even more familiar conflict scenario.

Complex church conflict is not new. In fact, the disciples didn't get much beyond the day of Pentecost before they experienced a notable episode in Acts.[7]

> During this time, as the disciples were increasing in numbers by leaps and bounds, hard feelings developed among the Greek-speaking believers—"Hellenists"—toward the Hebrew-speaking believers because their widows were being discriminated against in the daily food lines. (Acts 6:1 MSG)

We seem to assume that problems are most likely to arise during dysfunctional and undesirable circumstances, e.g., tough economic times, declining church attendance, spiritual carnality. However, this conflict erupted during a tremendous period of growth in the early church: "the disciples were increasing in numbers by leaps and bounds"! One commentator refers to this period as a "momentous advance in the community of Jesus followers."[8]

What about poor pastoral leadership or weak lay leaders? W. A. Criswell observes, "These were the men who had been taught by the Lord Himself. This is the church upon which God had poured out the ascension gift of the Holy Spirit. This is the church where the preaching of the Word was confirmed by signs and wonders."[9] Oh, but certainly only ingrown, shrinking, and self-focused churches invite the most serious conflicts, right? The last measurement cited in Scripture for the Jerusalem church was five thousand souls (Acts 4:4), but this meant at least twenty thousand people were there, including women and children. And there is every indication that the church was both missional in focus and clearly successful, as illustrated by the growing numbers of the Hellenistic Jews. Get the picture? Churches will have conflict even if they are the most productive, Spirit-filled, and biblical churches in the world!

Time for a Paradigm Shift

Negative, unhealthy conditions and behaviors often lead to church conflict. But rapid growth and desirable change usually bring trouble too! The question is not whether your church will experience conflict but rather what you will do when it comes. Although visible disagreements (presenting issues) are often the first symptoms to emerge, these incidents are not usually what is really causing the conflict. But we may be tempted to think, *If we just cajole people to forgive one another and to make nice, surely we can put this whole unhappy business behind us.* Seldom is this true. In my experience, virtually all interpersonal conflicts have an underlying root cause that is not immediately apparent.

If we are to transform painful crises into genuine breakthroughs, we must change the way we view conflict. Conflict avoidance and defensive reactions must be replaced with biblical insight and spiritual responsiveness. The "hard feelings" mentioned in Acts 6:1 can be replaced with a healthy curiosity and the expectation of God-given opportunities for growth.

Where to Start

Once church leaders can reframe their view of a situation from one of hopelessness to one of hopeful possibilities, they can begin to evaluate these "hard feelings" with new insight. This is where the Levels of Conflict diagram can become a tool to help church leaders sort things out. The "fog" can be lifted, and the geography of a conflicted situation can find better definition for healthy next steps.

Consider the example from Acts chapter 6 again. What are the presenting issues? Which conflicts might lie within the interpersonal level? Are there problems between groups or within groups? What about structural issues such as leadership deficits, cultural or cross-cultural concerns, and organizational factors? The matrix below illustrates how the problems in the early church at Jerusalem might be analyzed, separated, and categorized. When dealing with conflicts in your own congregation, you will have access to much more detail for evaluating a situation. Because of the brief description offered in the Scripture here, some assumptions will be made to add practical details for purposes of clarification.

PRESENTING ISSUE	CONFLICT LEVEL(S)	RATIONALE
"hard feelings developed among the Greek-speaking believers— 'Hellenists'—toward the Hebrew-speaking believers because their widows were being discriminated against in the daily food lines" (Acts 6:1 MSG).	**Intrapersonal** ("hard feelings") **Interpersonal** ("between" individuals) **Intragroup** (some differences of opinion within groups assumed) **Intergroup** (Hebrews/Hellenists) **Structural** (cultural, leadership, organizational issues)	Even though information here is limited, it is assumed that a conflict of this magnitude involved all of the conflict levels. "Hard feelings" implies both intra- and interpersonal issues. Two groups are mentioned but often factions develop within groups. Clearly the church was outgrowing its infrastructure and leadership and organizational changes were needed.

Turning to solutions

Holistic church conflict intervention requires crafting different intervention strategies for each of the different levels of conflict. Finding healthy solutions at each level requires recognizing and understanding an effective method and discrete strategies for each of these levels. Helping individuals with intrapersonal conflict is quite different from helping individuals with interpersonal conflict. Group interventions require approaches different from those for resolving structural issues. The interventions can sometimes be implemented simultaneously but should be evaluated for prioritization. The next verses in Acts 6 provide additional insights into how the apostles forged strategies at these different levels.

> The Twelve called a meeting of the disciples. They said, "It wouldn't be right for us to abandon our responsibilities for preaching and teaching the Word of God to help with the care of the poor. So, friends, choose seven men from among you whom everyone trusts, men full of the Holy Spirit and good sense, and we'll assign them this task. Meanwhile, we'll stick to our assigned tasks of prayer and speaking God's Word." (Acts 6:2–4 MSG)

In spite of sparse detail, Scripture provides significant clues into the apostles' thinking in the midst of a potential church-splitting crisis. Their words and actions indicate awareness and sensitivity to all five levels of church conflict. As we approach the practical matters of sorting out the issues and developing strategies for intervention, we would all do well to notice a foundational prerequisite for the apostolic method of decision-making prior to any action: their dependence on God's Spirit! In selecting a leadership team to tackle this challenge, the apostles stipulated that these individuals must be "men full of the Holy Spirit"! They also declared the primacy of the Word of God and prayer in their own leadership philosophy.

The congregation thought this was a great idea. They went ahead
and chose—Stephen, a man full of faith and the Holy Spirit, Philip,
Procorus, Nicanor, Timon, Parmenas, Nicolas, a convert from
Antioch. Then they presented them to the apostles. Praying, the
apostles laid on hands and commissioned them for their task.
    The Word of God prospered. The number of disciples in Jerusa-
lem increased dramatically. Not least, a great many priests submitted themselves to the faith. (Acts 6:5–7 MSG)

APOSTOLIC STRATEGY	CONFLICT LEVEL(S)	RATIONALE
Leadership Priorities: spiritual calling, maturity and gifting above all else.	**Intrapersonal** (heart first) **Interpersonal** ("everyone trusts")	We can only speculate on some of the details in this case but verse 7 suggests that successful resolution was accomplished at all five levels. When structural deficits are corrected, most of the other levels of conflict will either disappear or become much more easily resolved.
Team Qualification and Selection: Greek names of the seven suggests cross-cultural sensitivities.	**Intragroup** (need for unity assumed) **Intergroup** (fairness established for both Hebrew/ Hellenist widows)	
Organizational (infra-structural) changes and leadership delegation.	**Structural** (cultural, leadership, organizational issues)	

   The apostles did not ignore or avoid the conflict but took deci-
sive steps to understand and resolve the issues before them. They
made leadership and organizational (structural) changes. They recognized the cross-cultural nature of the problem and selected—
with the support of the congregation—men of spiritual maturity
and giftedness to minister to the needs at hand. Although we have
to speculate a little in light of the brevity of the account, the fact
that verse 7 indicates unhindered advancement of the church following this episode, we can assume that damaged relationships
were nurtured back to health again. We will be looking at biblical

principles and strategies for addressing all these levels in detail in the pages ahead.

EXERCISE

ANALYZING THE WHITE SANDS BIBLE CHURCH CONFLICT

Conducting good conflict analysis depends on gaining access to and evaluating adequate information. To begin to familiarize yourself with this process, reread the opening story of this chapter. Use the matrix below to begin sorting and categorizing the issues involved in this scenario. This exercise is designed to help you identify presenting issues and sort them into helpful categories. Don't worry about finding solutions at this point but only about identifying and separating issues. We will get to the solutions in the next chapters. To help locate these factors, simply ask yourself the following questions (see Appendix A to check your answers):

1. What are the presenting issues (most visible aspects)
   of this conflict? List in column A.
2. To which of the five conflict levels does each issue
   belong? List in column B.
3. Why did you place this issue in this level? List in column C.

At first, you may feel like the information that is surfacing with these probing questions is a bit overwhelming. Don't be discouraged! We will be walking through this process a step at a time in Section Three, and you will be amazed and encouraged at how helpful and simple the process becomes once you plug in your own situations and details. It will be encouraging because the sorting process clarifies and makes obvious the best next steps along the way. It will seem simple because the skills that are needed are the very same ones you already use in pastoral ministry every day—just with new applications.

(A) PRESENTING ISSUE(S)	(B) CONFLICT LEVEL(S)	(C) RATIONALE
1.	**Intrapersonal**	
2.		
3.	**Interpersonal**	
4.		
5.	**Intragroup**	
6.		
7.	**Intergroup**	
8.		
9.	**Structural**	
10.		

In the next chapter, we move to analyzing or mapping your conflict. You will learn how to distinguish between presenting issues and root causes as well as how to develop intervention strategies at each level.

Chapter 4

Mapping Your Conflict

We know that in all things God works for the good of those who love him, who have been called according to his purpose.
—Romans 8:28 NIV

It is the glory of God to conceal a matter; to search out a matter is the glory of kings.
—Proverbs 25:2 NIV

Pastor Jay Snowberger found himself in an unexpected season of disappointment, exhaustion, and depression at a time when he thought his pastoral ministry would be flourishing. He had spent thirty years enjoying ministry growth in a thriving church of which he was the founding pastor. *What is happening to me?* he wondered as he sat in his office one Sunday afternoon. His sense of God's calling and spiritual satisfaction was at an all-time low.

Jay is not alone. Many pastors find themselves in confusing places. After many years of ministry success, the very people they have served sacrificially for many years seem strangely unsupportive.

As he locked his office door and headed to the parking lot, Jay was questioning his calling, almost for the first time in his Christian ministry. Physically and spiritually, he felt burned out. Why didn't he see this coming, and why was he feeling helpless to change it? How could things have gone so painfully wrong?

As confusing as these circumstances were to Jay, the source of his predicament was really not hard to identify. All that was required was an objective process to sort out the issues and to map constructive steps to resolution.

Identify Presenting Issues

Jay's congregation and board were feeling confusion as well. But to an observant eye, patterns had been emerging that could have provided insight into both the surface issues and the root causes. Patterns are distinguished from single events, in that single episodes don't signify systemic issues. Repeated episodes with similar characteristics do and therefore are considered patterns.

As outlined before, we'll call the categories we have found most helpful in this process *levels of conflict*. We illustrate the process of "mapping" categories below. To simplify, we focus on the single issue that proved most significant for helping this pastor and his church. Once this main issue was identified and resolved, most of the other conflicts disappeared also. More will be said about this phenomenon in the next chapter covering *structural conflicts*.

As you read through these presenting issues, don't be too concerned if they seem disconnected or somewhat randomly listed. One frequent characteristic of presenting issues is that to the casual observer they seem quite unrelated to one another. It is roughly analogous to diagnosing a disease in the human body from seemingly unrelated symptoms. It is not until the physician discerns a particular pattern in the symptoms that the underlying disease can be finally identified. And the right treatment cannot be determined until the disease is accurately diagnosed. So it is in the body of the church.

INTRAPERSONAL	INTERPERSONAL	INTRAGROUP	INTERGROUP	STRUCTURAL
"Pastor Jay seems withdrawn and sometimes angry." "The head usher was reported for being rude to first-time visitors."	"There are conflicts between staff members and other church leaders." "Two Sunday school teachers were heard arguing in the foyer."	"The elder board is divided on the question of staff effectiveness." "The children's ministry leaders don't get along and are always begging for volunteers."	"The youth ministry and other ministry teams seem conflicted over financial resources." "The deacons and the elders seem conflicted in their roles and ineffective in their ministries."	"Pastor Jay doesn't seem effective or as passionate in his preaching as he used to be." "There seems to be great frustration among leaders in general."

Confusion and sadness were common among church members. Newer families seemed to question leadership competence. Others sensed that something was just not right.

As mentioned before, the observations in the chart may seem difficult to connect at first. This is often the case with presenting issues. So what might be the relationship between these observations: "Pastor Snowberger doesn't seem effective or as passionate in his preaching as he used to be" and "There seems to be great frustration among leaders in general"?

We might be tempted to conclude that the primary cause is some deficiency in the pastor himself. In fact, a number of leaders and members were thinking just that! Another common mistake in analyzing conflict is to look at the other categories or levels of comments in the conflict diagram and too quickly arrive at the conclusion that many of these observations may also reflect directly on Pastor Jay's leadership. Notice that this pastor's performance-related issues appear in both the Intrapersonal and Structural levels. Often when there are structural roots to a conflict, identifiable symptoms manifest on multiple levels. Therefore, although Jay Snowberger's performance is indeed suffering, it is premature to conclude that this is the *root* of the church's problems. So where do we go from here?

Discover Underlying (Root) Causes and Move toward Solutions

As confusing as these symptoms seem, please notice how simple and effective the solution is both to discover and to implement, once these symptoms are explored. One of Jay's closest colleagues, Dennis Simmons, pastor of a nearby church, invited him to a local coffee shop.

"I'm feeling really burned out," Jay confessed to his friend. "I just don't find any joy in my work these days," he added.

Dennis listened closely as his longtime friend talked about the gradual disenchantment that had occurred over many years in his ministry.

Dennis waited for a pause in Jay's words before speaking. "If you could wave a magic wand and change what you are doing in the church, what would you make different?" Dennis asked.

"That's easy; I'd get back to what I love—spending time with people instead of doing all this administrative work" was Jay's quick reply.

Dennis asked, "Does the leadership know how you feel?"

After a long hesitation, Jay said, "I'm not sure; we have not been communicating very well lately."

"Maybe you need an executive pastor or an administrative assistant," Dennis suggested.

Jay's spiritual gift profile identified *teaching* and *mercy* as his primary gifts and *administration* as his lowest. Over the years as this church grew in size and complexity, the need for *leadership* and *administration* gifts had increased dramatically. This particular denomination historically defines the senior pastor as the CEO of the organization. So two things happened as the church grew larger: Jay's capacity to lead a growing staff in an increasingly complex structure became overtaxed, and congregational satisfaction with his performance diminished.

By the time this conversation with Dennis occurred, Jay's duties had become painfully out of step with his gifting. He was spending 80 percent of his time in administration (his weakest gift) and only 20 percent in teaching and counseling (his strongest gifts). No wonder his performance was faltering!

When Jay realized what was happening, he met with the leadership to explain the growing disconnect between his job description and his God-given gifts. For the first time in years there was a breakthrough in understanding. His leaders were enthusiastic! It was decided to customize the senior pastor's job description so as to free Jay to use his primary gifts, and to hire an executive pastor to shift the load of these types of duties to someone more gifted in administration. Not only did these steps revitalize Jay's ministry and sense of calling, but it provided needed relief to the congregation by offering better structure and organizational leadership.

Most of the remaining conflicts quickly disappeared. The few that remained were easily resolved with coaching, counseling, and informal mediation. The new administrator was a former elder and retired businessman discovered within the congregation. Once this person was in place, Jay took some time off, and on his return was able to recover from near burnout within just a few months. In the end, recognizing and addressing this single root cause, which was structural (misalignment of the pastor's gifts with his job description), brought resolution to the perplexing array of seemingly unrelated presenting issues throughout the congregation.

Ocean Grove Community Church:
Moving to a More Challenging Opportunity

Bill Casey and James Cochran, officials with the denomination, sat with Pastor Drew Reynolds in a restaurant on a cold, rainy night in the Northwest. They had just arrived after a long drive to assist one of their regional congregations whose leaders had asked for help. Pastor Drew appeared reticent and insecure as he explained recent events at Ocean Grove Community Church. "It's been devastating," he said quietly, as if ashamed to speak about it. The church had been running around a thousand in total worship attendance only six months before. This past Sunday, it was closer to five hundred.

What Pastor Drew described was indeed an ugly scene. More than half the church's staff had either been terminated or had resigned in the past six months. The elders had dismissed the senior pastor and, as associate pastor with an absent senior pastor, Drew Reynolds was now serving as the default leader of a broken congregation with a divided elder board. Gossip was rampant. Widespread distrust made things even worse. Bill and James were about to learn why things had so rapidly deteriorated and to witness, over the next few months, an amazing transformation.

Bill and James interviewed the remaining staff members, whose descriptions of church life couldn't have been more disheartening. The associate pastor, Drew, in the absence of the senior pastor, had been the one to preside over most of the recent staff departures. The children's ministry and youth pastors were fired, and the Christian education pastor resigned just a few months later. When asked about the status of those individuals, fears of recrimination and even litigation surfaced. When they invited Drew's perspectives on the reasons for the conflict, a confusing array of seemingly unrelated events were cited. And to make matters worse, some members of the congregation mistakenly believed that the constitution and bylaws required denominational approval to terminate the senior pastor. These members were adding fuel to the flames through gossip and innuendo. The next step was to interview members of the congregation.

Presenting issues

In assisting congregations in his denominational district, Bill Casey typically invited churches to put sign-up sheets in the lobby several weeks before his arrival. The invitation for interviews was extended to anyone in attendance who wished to schedule a meeting. About a hundred people at Ocean Grove Community Church signed up. The following is a summary of representative comments they made. Although they are sorted into categories below, this separation of issues was done by Bill and James afterward when they returned to their motel rooms. During these interviews, they simply gathered as much data as possible. Some comments appear in more than one category (level). That is because the issue potentially impacts multiple levels. Don't worry if you fail to see connections initially, as these will become apparent as we move forward in the process and explain more about these as we go along.

INTRAPERSONAL	INTERPERSONAL	INTRAGROUP	INTERGROUP	STRUCTURAL
1. "I heard from one of its members that the elder board is divided." 2. "I hear gossip and character assassination regularly in the hallways on Sunday mornings." 3. "One of the former pastoral staff members is starting a new church in his home."	1. "Rob and Jack (elders) were seen arguing in public." 2. "Two deacons were seen arguing about elder issues in the parking lot." 3. "Ryanne (a deaconess) said she was deeply hurt by Deb (women's ministry leader)."	1. "The trustees had a big fight over installing a computer system in the building." 2. "The children's ministry leaders don't get along and are always short of volunteers." 3. "Some people won't talk to other people; they even sit on different sides of the sanctuary."	1. "The elder board had an emergency meeting to review some of the staff conflict and reprimanded one staff member for recent conduct." 2. "The deacons and the elders seem confused in their roles and are ineffective in their ministries."	1. "The associate pastor didn't have the authority to terminate the two staff members." 2. "The constitution was violated when the elder board didn't contact the denominational leadership prior to both the termination of the senior pastor and of other staff by the associate pastor." 3. "I took my concerns to the pastor, and nothing was ever done." 4. "I heard from one of its members that the elder board is divided."

Discovering root causes

Notice again how scattered the visible issues appear to be. Remember that presenting issues are frequently just symptoms of deeper concerns. The next step is to identify patterns and underlying causes to these symptoms. This will inform our strategy when we begin to design interventions at each level.

To simplify the matrix above, the comments will be broken down and discussed one level at a time. Through my observations in similar cases, these conclusions are well supported even if the brief descriptions provided here seem insufficient to explain those circumstances completely. Because these issues overlap, multiple layers may be involved and are noted in parentheses as applicable.

The bold print below depicts the presenting issue, and the comment that follows indicates possible root causes and noted impacts in additional levels. When we get to designing interventions, these issues will be separated so they can be addressed appropriately. One of the most important things to understand is that unless this type of analysis is done, root causes remain hidden and therefore continue to cause conflicts. Again, please don't let the apparent chaos in this conflict fool you. The beauty of this tool is how this sorting process can lead to clarity, understanding, and good decision-making in finding sustainable solutions.

Intrapersonal Level

1. **"I heard from one of its members that the elder board is divided."**

   This comment suggests both a character issue for the elder (as evidenced by his violation of the board's confidentiality agreement) and a gossip problem by the non-board member, which is also intrapersonal.

2. **"I hear gossip and character assassination regularly in the hallways on Sunday mornings."**

The gossip issue appears to be widespread, pointing to an organization-wide cultural issue (structural/systemic).

3. **"One of the former pastoral staff members is starting a new church in his home."**

In this particular denomination, this action constitutes a pastoral ethical violation (character issue) with consequences in the intergroup level potentially involving both congregations (intergroup) and also involves the district (structural/systemic level).

Interpersonal Level

1. **"Rob and Jack (elders) were seen arguing in public."**

This appears to be an interpersonal conflict between Rob and Jack, which is the presenting issue. But underneath, it was discovered that the root cause to this argument stemmed from deficits that were both intrapersonal (character-related issues) and leadership training issues (structural/systemic).

2. **"Two deacons were seen arguing about elder issues in the parking lot."**

Beyond revealing the interpersonal presenting issue between these two deacons, underlying issues reflect board tensions (intragroup) and across groups (intergroup), and impact the entire organization leadership structure (structural/systemic).

3. **"Ryanne (a deaconess) said she was deeply hurt by Deb (women's ministry leader)."**

Although different people and groups are involved here, the same issues as listed above are at play.

Intragroup and Intergroup Levels

(These two levels are combined here to simplify and save space, but the differences between them become significant when designing intervention methods. This will be covered when we address resolution strategies. For these reasons, some examples cited on the matrix are not included here because they represent duplication of similar issues or were already cited above. They will be included in the intervention design section.)

1. **"The trustees had a big fight over installing a computer system in the building."**

   This presenting issue surfaced as a disagreement within the trustee board. However, further investigation revealed that this board division actually had roots in mistrust of certain leaders and in procedural decision-making questions (structural/systemic).

2. **"The deacons and the elders seem confused in their roles and are ineffective in their ministries."**

   This conflict between leadership boards revealed role confusion, causing members of both boards to feel undervalued at times and intruded on at others. This represented both leadership and policy deficits (structural/systemic issues).

3. **"Some people won't talk to other people; they even sit on different sides of the sanctuary."**

   Factions had formed within the congregation over unspecified issues. Most of these factions dissolved when solutions were implemented on the structural level issues.

Structural/Systemic Level

1. **"The associate pastor didn't have authority to terminate the two staff members he fired after the senior pastor was terminated."**

   This resulted from a lack of policy clarity on administrative procedures when the senior pastor position was vacant.

2. **"The constitution was violated when the elder board didn't contact the denominational leadership prior to both the**

termination of the senior pastor by the board and of other staff by the associate pastor."
Although this accusation sounds similar to the one above, it actually represented tensions that developed between the congregational leadership and the denominational superintendent. There was a lack of trust and clarity on administrative procedure as related to the denominational role in local churches during times of conflict.

3. **"I took my concerns to the pastor, and nothing was ever done."**
Investigation of this complaint turned out to be very significant in a number of cultural issues within the church as related to the absence of legitimate channels for communication.

4. **"I heard from one of its members that the elder board is divided."**
Both the gossip component and the confidentiality breach needed to be addressed.

Design Holistic Intervention Strategies

Bill and James now had the information they needed to begin working with church leaders on good solutions. This initial analysis led to a number of effective intervention strategies. The steps they recommended are summarized in the table below. In Section Three, we will provide more details in how these steps can be implemented and how the outcomes can benefit the church.

INTRAPERSONAL	INTERPERSONAL	INTRAGROUP	INTERGROUP	STRUCTURAL/SYSTEMIC
Intrapersonal conflicts are often best addressed in counseling, coaching, discipleship, and/or training sessions (individual and group).	Interpersonal conflict resolution principles should follow those outlined in Matthew 18 and can include negotiation, mediation, and arbitration sessions.	Facilitated problem-solving sessions can be designed in various ways depending on group size and dynamics.	Similar methods to those used in facilitating within groups can also be helpful when working between groups.	Organizational leaders are the most common participants for making structural/systemic decisions and changes. Outside coaching can often be helpful in this process.

The transformation that took place in the following months at Ocean Grove Community Church exceeded Bill and James's wildest expectations! Although the process was painful at times and took more than a year, the church found encouragement in seeing progress and unity strengthened as the members of the congregation worked together. Significant numerical growth took place also. God honored this congregation's transparency, determination, and faithful obedience.

No small amount of credit goes to a leadership team, including an interim pastor who was called during this process at the recommendation of the district superintendent. This team proved willing to face their fears and change their behaviors in order to become a model for the entire congregation. However, they also benefited significantly from a systematic analysis of their situation and a strategic intervention plan to address every issue they identified. The structural changes had the biggest impact. In the next chapter we will dig deeper into helping church leaders understand the importance of this level of church conflict, both from an analytical perspective and in the design phase toward healthy solutions.

Chapter 5

Structural Conflict

*Paul insisted that they should not take with them the one
who had departed from them in Pamphylia, and had not gone
with them to the work. Then the contention became so sharp that
they parted from one another. And so Barnabas took
Mark and sailed to Cyprus; but Paul chose Silas and departed, being
commended by the brethren to the grace of God.*
— Acts 15:38–40 NKJV

*A church crisis often creates a brief open window
during which the leaders are open to making major
changes in their priorities, actions, and personal lives,
that they normally might not be willing to consider.*[10]
— Eddy Hall

"We just can't continue to run this community children's program
any longer," Jodie stated flatly. She was speaking of a long-standing
youth outreach program that had been a centerpiece of the church's
youth outreach ministry for decades.

Then Del spoke up, agreeing. "It is just so labor intensive! We
can't find enough volunteers to cover the bases any longer. We
need volunteers in all our ministries, and there aren't enough to
go around."

The board members around the table sat in silence, and with no
objections, everyone appeared to agree. There seemed to be a collec-
tive sigh of resignation—as if to say, "This is the right thing to do."

The Christian education board of Faith Church is composed of
members from all the church's educational departments, including adult and youth ministry. However, representatives from each
program in the department are not required to attend monthly

meetings. So there was no one from this specific children's out-reach group in attendance. Instead, one person representing the entire youth ministry was present. With no further discussion, the decision to cancel this program carried unanimously and was duly noted in the minutes. Little did this group of volunteer leaders realize what a firestorm this well-intentioned decision was about to unleash in their church!

As soon as word got out that the program was slated for cancellation, phones started to ring and both volunteers and parents were in an uproar. Pastor Marshall Davison was just about to turn in for the night when an angry church member called him at home. Marshall knew a Christian Ed board meeting was taking place but was unprepared for the alarm that was sounding throughout much of his congregation.

He hurriedly called a combined elder board and Christian education board meeting for the following evening to try and head off any further trouble. It was too late. By the time the elders and the Christian education board met the next day, many in the congregation had taken sides on the issue and more than a few were threatening to leave the church. This children's ministry had been central in the lives of many longtime church members and was even the reason some families had joined. How could these leaders be so out of touch? Why was there not one objection to a decision affecting so many?

As often happens, much of the hurt and anger was quickly personalized, and the resulting polarization centered on people instead of issues. Those feeling hurt and rejected needed someone to blame, and the Christian Ed board was not the only vulnerable target. Many assumed the elders and the pastor were implicit in this decision. Blame was even spilling over onto their spouses! A church split seemed inevitable, unless something could be done to turn the tide quickly.

Fortunately, in this case something was done quickly. The elders met with the Christian education board to better understand how the decision was made. The leaders who made the decision realized their error of not including leaders involved in this children's program in the decision-making process. Another meeting with volunteer staff and parents was hurriedly scheduled, and the board members acknowledged their shortsightedness and apologized publicly. They reversed their decision.

It took a few weeks for people to settle down, but a big turning point came in identifying the root cause of this painful experience. The source of this near calamity was not to be found in sinful intentions or malicious actions but in gaps in organizational communication. Structural adjustments were needed to prevent similar mistakes from occurring in the future. Once these changes were made, communication improved and better decision-making ensued. There was peace again at Faith Church, and a very important lesson was learned.

Organizational Deficits

Structural factors are usually the most highly significant and the least recognizable sources of conflict in the church. As observed in Acts 6, the conflicts surfaced first in interpersonal and intergroup disputes. However, solutions were not found until the leadership deficits, cultural misalignments, and spiritual needs were identified, addressed, and implemented. The early church's infrastructure was inadequate to accommodate their rapid growth and diversity. Godly leaders listened to the Holy Spirit and were able to recognize needed changes in leadership and structures. Once done, the early church continued its phenomenal ministry!

CULTURAL ISSUES AT
MOUNTAIN SHADOWS FELLOWSHIP

"I can't worship with that noise!" Henry said, disgusted. Mountain Shadows Fellowship was about to add a second Sunday morning service offering a contemporary worship band. This church had long been known for its conservative approach to ministry including a history of using traditional hymns in worship. Although a number of congregational meetings took place, Henry and a number of other tenured church members were not present at these.

People often think of national or ethnic differences when they hear the word "culture." But *culture* is a much broader term than that. All organizational groups, including churches, have distinctive cultural attributes. Culture has been defined as "the symbolic and learned aspects of human society."[11] Church life can embrace a rich and diverse array of theological, historical, ethnic, economic, political, and demographic factors, among others. Although passages such as Romans 12 and 1 Corinthians 12 teach that such differences within the body of Christ (especially as related to the spiritual gifts) are meant to bring unity through diversity, too often these differences bring only division and conflict.

In my experience, 90 percent of the underlying causes of organizational conflict have structural roots, and many times these factors are cultural in nature. The worship wars[12] have been a common source of church division for decades.

In the example from the early Jerusalem church, all these cultural categories were present. The differences between Jewish and Gentile believers included historical, ethnic, religious, and economic factors, among others. In most churches today, congregations consist of people from varied ethnic, demographic, economic, political, and religious backgrounds.

LEADERSHIP CHALLENGES AT
OCEAN GROVE COMMUNITY CHURCH

The last chapter demonstrated how the differing levels of church conflict could be analyzed and separated. This example will serve to illustrate how leadership issues can factor into both church conflict and finding good solutions. (Refer to the case study beginning on page 59.) Sorting out issues into these five categories (Intrapersonal, Interpersonal, Intragroup, Intergroup, and Structural) makes the next steps toward finding good solutions much easier. The secret to not being overwhelmed when faced with complex organizational conflict is to break down the elements into understandable bite-sized pieces that can be addressed one at a time. Now let's look at how good conflict analysis helps these church leaders design and implement strategic interventions into the Ocean Grove church conflict. The process begins here with the structural issues and then moves to other levels in future chapters.

STRUCTURAL/SYSTEMIC ISSUES

1. "The associate pastor didn't have authority to terminate the two staff members he fired after the senior pastor was terminated."

2. "The constitution was violated when the elder board didn't contact the denominational leadership prior to firing the senior pastor."

3. "I took my concerns to the pastor and nothing was ever done."

4. "I heard from one of its members that the elder board is divided."

STRUCTURAL/SYSTEMIC PROBLEM SOLVING

Organizational leaders are the most common participants for making structural/systemic decisions and changes. Outside coaching can often be helpful in this process also.

Structural/systemic level
problems and resolution strategies

1. **"The associate pastor didn't have authority to terminate the two staff members he fired after the senior pastor was terminated."**

This resulted from a lack of policy clarity on administrative procedures when the senior pastor position was vacant. With the associate pastor cast into deep water by a dysfunctional and divided governing board, emotions ran high and decision-making was hurried and inconsistent. A general lack of knowledge, both of the denomination's policies and regarding best practices for resolving personnel issues, led to mishandled terminations of staff. In addition, the church's written policy manual was too brief and lacked sufficient detail to guide less experienced staff and board members through this process.

Denominational resources existed to help local churches with these matters but had not been consulted. Now, with the district leaders involved, adequate information and training could be received to avoid these types of missteps in the future. A seasoned human resources professional within the congregation was identified and stepped forward to advise the staff and the board on future personnel questions. Church documents were amended to incorporate these improved policies and procedures, and leadership training was implemented for current and future leaders to attend.

2. **"The constitution was violated when the elder board didn't contact the denominational leadership prior to firing the senior pastor."**

It turns out that this accusation was not accurate because the church's governing documents did not address the matter of denominational involvement in local congregations, except in matters of doctrinal infidelity. Although this accusation sounds similar to the previous one, it actually represented tensions that had developed between some of the congregational leaders and the denominational superintendent. There was a lack of trust and clarity on administrative procedure as related to the denominational role in local churches during times of conflict. These tensions were alleviated through healthy facilitated problem-solving sessions convened by these denominational officials at the request of the interim pastor. Good relations between the denominational and church leaders were restored.

3. "I took my concerns to the pastor and nothing was ever done." Investigation of this complaint by Bill and James from the denomination revealed the absence of legitimate channels for communication within the congregation. Because of a conflict avoidance culture modeled by the leaders and adopted by the congregation, serious gaps existed in healthy communication generally. When legitimate channels of communication are lacking within organizations, it is not uncommon for illegitimate ones to develop. Gossip and slander become the avenues of choice for many.

During the resolution process, the interim pastor humbly acknowledged the failure of church leadership to listen to and to communicate effectively with the congregation. He led the creation of new methods for receiving feedback from members and channels to report needed information back to the congregation. Further, he preached a series of messages on gossip, edifying communication principles, and biblical conflict resolution guidelines from Matthew 18. A behavioral covenant was created between the staff, board, and congregation, including biblical teaching on preventing gossip through redirecting people to engage the individuals with whom they experienced conflicts.

4. "I heard from one of its members that the elder board is divided."

The gossip component is addressed above. The confidentiality breach was addressed through requiring all current and future staff and board members to adopt and sign a confidentiality agreement.

These structural changes had an immediate impact on the entire congregation. Gossip greatly diminished, and those who failed to comply soon lost credibility and influence. People began to actively recognize illegitimate, sinful behaviors and refused to participate in gossip. Instead they began to redirect violators to practice Matthew 18 principles.

Greater transparency of leaders combined with healthy communication methods rebuilt trust. Pastors, board members, and the entire congregation began to heal. As these organizational improvements took hold, the culture of Ocean Grove Community Church was transformed. The worship services became joyful again! The majority of problems involving interpersonal and intergroup conflict within the church disappeared. However, some relationships were so damaged during church conflict that even after the larger issues were resolved, more needed to be done. Counseling, coaching, mediation, and facilitated problem-solving brought resolution over several months.

A Word about Nested Conflicts[13]

"Can we talk?" Jared requested quietly.

"Sure," Stan replied. "Let's go to my office right after this meeting."

Stan and Jared serve on the pastoral staff of Westcliff Fellowship Church and were just finishing up a staff meeting, which was led by the senior pastor, Rick Brown. Jared heads a group of volunteer high school workers in a thriving youth ministry, and Stan is the administrative pastor of this large congregation in Milwaukee. Both men had served together on staff for over ten years, knew each other well, and enjoyed a trusting friendship as well as a good working relationship.

As they sat down in Stan's office, Jared looked concerned but seemed hesitant to speak. After a few awkward moments of small talk, he said, "Stan, I'm not sure what to do." Both men sat quietly for several seconds before Jared continued.

"Our youth ministry seems to be going great, but not everyone is happy. Janelle has stopped speaking to me and always seems upset when I see her."

Janelle led a large and successful middle and junior high school ministry and had done so for as long as anyone could remember.

"So what's going on, Jared?" Stan asked.

"I'm concerned about something Janelle told me, and I warned her that she is headed for real trouble."

"What's this about?" Stan was growing impatient.

"Well, quite honestly, I think that she is violating church policies and is definitely operating unethically," Jared told Stan.

"Wow, I'm not sure you should be telling *me* this; have you let Janelle know how serious your concerns are?"

"I have," Jared replied, "and she got upset with me. I told her that if she didn't come forward and tell you or Pastor Rick, I would do so myself."

"Does Janelle know you're talking with me about this today?" Stan asked.

"Yes. She told me to mind my own business, but I told her yesterday was the deadline and offered to come with her if she would report her activities. She refused. But she knows I'm here," Jared replied.

"Okay, what exactly is going on?" Stan said, trying to move the conversation forward.

"She's done a great job of outreach," Jared said. "Many of the kids involved in our junior high ministry are from non-Christian homes. But an increasing number are being recruited from other churches. I'm thrilled she has a heart to help them, but she isn't notifying parents in many cases that their kids are participating or even where they are!"

———————◆———————

Nested conflict theory suggests that in organizational conflicts, there can be overlapping levels of conflict as related to existing subsystems. In other words, in our model, this would be one way to view numerous conflicts arising on different levels within the model but sharing a common root cause. In the case just described (at Westcliff Fellowship Church), the first visible sign of conflict (presenting issue) was most likely the conflict between Jared and Janelle (interpersonal level).

However, there is also conflict within and between the high school and middle school teams (intra- and intergroup conflict). Within and between these teams is confusion regarding outreach policies and standards. And the root cause (and most strategic) level of conflict is structural in nature. Until leadership addresses the ethical and policy issues involved, no sustainable resolution can be realized.

Unfortunately, in many cases like this one, the interpersonal dynamics along with sinful responses combine to escalate already volatile circumstances. This illustrates how important it can be to recognize potential or emerging conflict as soon as it surfaces and begin opening lines of communication, starting the analysis process, and engaging the needs as they arise. Several triggers are already visible, providing immediate opportunities to act:

1. Jared has done the right thing by attempting to confront Janelle one-on-one, assuming it was done in a loving and respectful manner.
2. We know that Janelle refused to bring forth the issues as requested to senior leadership and that is why Jared has now come to Stan, the administrative pastor.
3. A good next step would be for Stan and Jared to attempt to set up a meeting with the three of them or, in some circumstances,[14] Janelle's direct supervisor.

As this case illustrates, conflict can exist on different levels and overlap. In the next chapter, we will move from addressing structural conflict and look more deeply into methods of resolving group conflict.

Chapter 6

Group and Intergroup Conflict

*An argument arose among them
as to which of them was the greatest.*
—Luke 9:46

*Some men came down from Judea and were teaching the
brothers, "Unless you are circumcised according to the custom
of Moses, you cannot be saved." And after Paul and Barnabas had
no small dissension and debate with them, Paul and Barnabas
and some of the others were appointed to go up to Jerusalem
to the apostles and the elders about this question.*
—Acts 15:1–2

"Jake and Sue Duncan have an amazing gift for working with teenagers!" Winston said, enthused.

"I couldn't agree more," Pastor Jeff replied. "Since Jake and Sue came, we've seen the youth ministry explode with new kids."

"I just don't know how they do it; they're like kid magnets," Winston said with a chuckle.

Jeff had only recently been called as the new solo pastor of Dawkins Valley Chapel and was thrilled to see things moving along so well with the youth ministry, especially under the leadership of this young couple.

It was an amazing development for this small, struggling congregation. An added benefit was seeing parents step forward in unprecedented numbers to volunteer to help with the youth ministry. Evidently the excitement that they were seeing in their own children was contagious. And this was not just true for the regular attendees. The influx of new families to the church was no doubt a part of this phenomenon. Teenagers inviting their friends from outside the church only added to the momentum. And it seemed that even when unchurched parents saw their children "wanting" to go to church, they, too, wanted to see what the attraction was all about.

But just when it seemed like things could only get better at Dawkins Valley Chapel, a small dark cloud appeared on the horizon.

Intragroup Conflict
(Involving Just One Group)

"What are Jake and Sue planning for the youth group these days?" Sophie asked. Sophie's two junior high students attended youth group activities regularly.

Beth, whose son is also in the group, replied, "I'm not really sure. Maybe we should ask Bill and Joyce. They volunteer at most of the youth group functions."

That Wednesday night, Beth called Joyce to see what she could learn. "Hi, Joyce, do you have time for a quick question about the youth group?" Beth asked.

"Sure," Joyce replied. "What's up?"

"My son absolutely loves being in youth group," Beth said, "and I really appreciate what you and Bill are doing to help out. But I have a hard time getting any information about what the group is planning as far as activities. Do you have a schedule or something?"

"Bill and I are only there on a rotating basis," Joyce said. "And to be honest, we never know what's going to happen until we get there. I'll call around to see what I can learn."

The series of phone calls that followed revealed a growing dissatisfaction among both parents and youth group volunteers regarding Jake and Sue's leadership. It became clear that an increasing number of these adults were feeling uneasy about a number of unknowns related to this youth ministry.

When Pastor Jeff heard what was happening, he quickly set up a meeting with Jake and Sue.

"Thanks for coming. I just need to check on a few things with you two," Pastor Jeff began.

"Sure, what do you want to know?" Jake asked.

The discussion revealed two things. First, this couple really loved working with the kids. And second, Jake and Sue were operating pretty much independently, without much communication with either the parents or volunteers. A pretty simple problem to solve, or so the pastor thought. However, what happened next was alarming. In spite of the success of these youth leaders, a church conflict was already developing.

Within a few weeks, the youth ministry at Dawkins Valley Chapel imploded. The team of volunteer parents fragmented and polarized, some fiercely supportive, others calling for the Duncans' heads. Pastor Jeff, after unsuccessfully attempting to mediate a number of the disputes and trying to save strained relationships, was forced to release the Duncans from their positions as volunteer youth leaders. Jake and Sue, perplexed and brokenhearted, left the church. This talented couple's dynamic relationship with the kids was now ended, and much of the growth that had occurred under their leadership quickly disappeared. What had happened? How could so much be lost so quickly?

Underutilizing available resources

The conflicts that destroyed the youth ministry at Dawkins Valley Chapel initially began inside one team. But that discontent quickly spread throughout the congregation. In hindsight, the dysfunction that caused this collapse should have been prevent-able. A church health consulting group was invited to interview the pastor, volunteers, parents, and kids, and the root causes were quickly identified as residing in weak organizational structure and poor communication.

Ironically, a wealth of talent and spiritual gifting was discovered to be present among the parent volunteers. A tenured church consultant once told me that in his experience, "people who are amazingly competent in their professional lives seem to forget everything they know and become complete idiots at church." Although he was obviously speaking tongue-in-cheek, he revealed a most unfortunate reality in many congregations. People who have great experience and skill in any number of disciplines (e.g., human resources, administration, communication, and others) may not utilize their talents at church. When their knowledge and experience could help church leaders, they seem mysteriously silent.

In this case, parents and volunteers were identified who were clearly gifted in organization, discernment, teaching, and serving and who could have easily assisted Jake and Sue in planning, communicating, and administrating the youth ministry effectively. But instead of helping make a great ministry even more remarkable, they stood on the sidelines, were swept up in the controversies, and became part of the problem instead of becoming part of the solution.

Early intervention

If Pastor Jeff (or other leaders) had initiated healthy conflict resolution steps earlier, the outcomes could have been positive. Leaders working in healthy church cultures learn to recognize conflict symptoms early and become proactive. Suppose the pastor or a parent or a youth volunteer leader had engaged Jake and Sue at the first sign of trouble. Further imagine that a healthy and constructive discussion followed. Because we are talking about a conflict with more than a few individuals, a problem-solving facilitation methodology would most likely be the best approach (see Section Three). If initiated early, instead of a session like this being characterized as a problem-solving one, it could have been a "brainstorming" or "planning" session, which can be more inviting than using words like "conflict" or "problem" in the announcement.

Imagine that Jake and Sue had welcomed parents and volunteers into this collaboration meeting to discuss and create a written plan so everyone could get on the same page and gain ownership. If Jake and/or Sue are not skilled facilitators, perhaps the pastor, another skilled church member, or even an outside facilitator could have led the process.

Depending on existing church policy documents, topics such as philosophy of ministry, policies and procedures, and spiritual standards could be discussed and decided on. When controversial subjects are anticipated or encountered, one simple method to help depressurize the meeting is to separate the discussion and decision-making sessions into two different meetings. These meetings should be scheduled to take place within an appropriate time frame for people to process what they are hearing. If the number of parents and volunteers is larger than about a dozen, then selecting a representative team of twelve or fewer can make the process more manageable and productive.

SAMPLE ISSUES THAT MIGHT ARISE IN A MEETING LIKE THIS	POSSIBLE STRATEGIES THAT MIGHT BE RECOMMENDED FOR RESOLUTION
1. What is our discipleship philosophy and methodology for training our youth? 2. What qualifications are required for our youth leaders and volunteers? 3. What teaching topics, texts, and/or curriculum will be used for junior and senior high youth? 4. What activities for these groups might be acceptable to our church and to their parents? 5. What guidelines will be established for individual and group behaviors in public and private? 6. What guidelines will we follow for off-site trips and activities? 7. What type of planning and scheduling needs to be done and communicated to our constituency? 8. Who will be responsible for each action item agreed on and in what time frame will each one be completed?	Depending on the level of conflict present before and during these meetings, strategies and methodologies should be carefully selected and then modified if circumstances change. Not infrequently, additional issues residing at different levels in the model arise in these sessions. If the group is small, these topics can often be addressed with the entire group. If it is a larger group, subteams may need to be created to focus on each significant topic and then brought back to the whole group. Specific directions and tools for addressing a host of variables like these are presented in Section Three of this book.

Intergroup Conflict
(Involving More than One Group)

In the last chapter, the division occurring at Mountain Shadows Fellowship over music styles serves as an example of cultural conflict which is a structural level conflict within our model. But as has already been demonstrated, one of the realities of complex organizational conflict is an overlapping of categories (nested conflict) that can be confusing in the fog of war that surrounds these types of disputes.

Even though worship wars almost always include cultural dynamics, they also involve at least two distinct factions (or groups) that make the dispute also an intergroup conflict. In the case of

Mountain Shadows, these groups were primarily generationally aligned—the older members of the congregation preferred traditional hymns and the younger people preferred praise choruses and worship songs.

Recognizing both the cultural distinctives and group dynamics of this conflict helped these church leaders understand the multiple issues involved and create an effective intervention strategy. In the Mountain Shadows case, trusted representatives from both sides of the issue were identified and invited to a collaborative brainstorming meeting early in the planning stages of beginning a second service that would feature contemporary music.

Although Henry and some of his close friends did not attend any of these sessions, others who felt just as strongly on both sides of this issue came, participated, and helped find common ground that ultimately united the church around more important missional objectives. The pastor was able to reframe the discussion and raise the dialogue above simply a question of defending personal music preferences to an elevated focus on the Great Commission.

This approach led to both groups coming together around a new paradigm characterized as "bilingual" outreach. However, in this case *bilingual* did not refer to two languages. Instead, music was presented as a cultural distinctive that spoke powerfully to each group in their own music language. The older generation began to see the potential of a new worship service as an outreach to the next generation and beyond (including their grandchildren!). The younger representatives realized a great open door to reach out to their unchurched friends, neighbors, and colleagues. But they also learned cross-generationally to appreciate and value the importance of the traditional hymns to the senior members of their congregation. Once this common vision was forged, selected church leaders were assigned to arrange home visits with church members in their own age groups to present and explain this new outreach philosophy and opportunity. Although a few individuals were not completely happy with the final decision, more than twenty years later there has never been any significant division in this church over worship music styles!

Next, we move from this discussion of group conflict to the very important matter of helping people resolve interpersonal conflict.

Chapter 7

Interpersonal Conflict Part One: People

While they were worshiping the Lord and fasting, the Holy Spirit said, "Set apart for me Barnabas and Saul for the work to which I have called them." Then after fasting and praying they laid their hands on them and sent them off.
—Acts 13:2–3

After some days Paul said to Barnabas, "Let us return and visit the brothers in every city where we proclaimed the word of the Lord, and see how they are." Now Barnabas wanted to take with them John called Mark. But Paul thought best not to take with them one who had withdrawn from them in Pamphylia and had not gone with them to the work. And there arose a sharp disagreement, so that they separated from each other. Barnabas took Mark with him and sailed away to Cyprus, but Paul chose Silas and departed, having been commended by the brothers to the grace of the Lord. And he went through Syria and Cilicia, strengthening the churches.
—Acts 15:36–41

Personality Issues

"We've been working together for how long? And you still manage to disappoint me on a regular basis!" Garry was almost shouting as he and his assistant pastor were supposed to be having their weekly update meeting.

Daniel paused to gather his thoughts. "Garry, we've been down this road so many times I just don't know how to talk to you.

Granted, you do a better job than I do when it comes to planning things out and keeping track of details. But I get the job done and, as far as I know, you're the only one concerned about my way of doing things! Why can't you just let me be me and you take care of your own part of all of this? We don't have to do everything exactly the same way."

"Personality conflict"

Conflicts almost always surface first in the level of interpersonal conflict, which can have many causes. Regardless of the root cause of a conflict, helping people navigate the interpersonal dynamics of their own relationships is essential to bringing resolution to the main issue(s) and reconciling people to one another.

Sometimes interpersonal conflict represents a single issue and can be resolved with no further action required. "Personality conflicts" often fall into this category. These words are in quotation marks because the suggestion that a conflict is primarily a difference in personalities is usually an oversimplification. God created us in His image and gifted us in different ways.

Garry and Daniel have been working together for more than five years. Both have been effective in their respective roles. But their different ministry and communication styles have led to a pattern of recurring conflict that has kept their relationship strained and even combative at times. These two men are wired (gifted) differently. Garry scores high in the area of administration, and Daniel's strongest gift is mercy. Garry is a detail person who enjoys making lists and completing tasks daily, while Daniel is highly relational and would rather go with the flow and make midcourse adjustments as needed. Garry plans and executes with efficiency and organizational excellence. Daniel is warm and welcoming and has built an amazing network of relationships across the entire ministry. Their gifts have complemented each other, bringing a healthy balance to the church's ministries. But their inability to work well together is now causing division within their leadership team. If it continues, churchwide conflict is inevitable.

Emotional control

God created emotions. When He said in Genesis that all He created was good, we can be sure our emotions were designed to be a source of great blessing to us and to those around us. However, in our fallen state, our emotions are subject to the frailties of the flesh. A common assumption is that our emotions are just a part of who we are and therefore should be allowed their full expression. But just like everything else in our lives, our emotions must be submitted to the control of the Holy Spirit. We must each resist the temptation to let uncontrolled emotions drive our decision-making. If we fail to form new habits shaped by scriptural principles, our emotions can fuel an explosive fire that causes us to respond to disagreements and challenges in ways that lead only to regret. Paul reminds us in Galatians 5:24 that "those who belong to Christ Jesus have crucified the flesh with its passions and desires," and Solomon teaches, "A man without self-control is like a city broken into and left without walls" (Prov. 25:28).

Spiritual formation

So how can church leaders help themselves and their congregations become skilled in healthy communication and problem-solving?

Although this book is intended to provide a workable model for resolving personal and systemic conflict, it is a mistake to think that mere mechanical methods and organizational processes are sufficient to bring about Christ-honoring solutions in the fullest sense. Proverbs 4:23 admonishes us to "above all else, guard your heart, for everything you do flows from it" (NIV). Improving our

skills in communication and conflict resolution are not simply aca-
demic exercises but part of our personal growth toward spiritual
maturity. As Proverbs says, "A man without self-control is like a
city broken into and left without walls" (25:28). For church leaders, this point is particularly relevant (1 Peter 5:1–3). Modeling
emotional self-control, especially in times of disagreement and
conflict, can make the difference between inspiring others toward
godly behavior or contributing to a devastating loss of credibility
and influence. Spiritual formation (character) is a lifelong process
that manifests itself most clearly in times of trouble. In *Renovation
of the Heart*, Dallas Willard observed,

> *Spiritual formation . . . is the process by which the human spirit or will
> is given a definite "form" or character.* It is a process that happens to
> everyone. . . . Terrorists as well as saints are the outcome of spiritual
> formation. Their spirits or hearts have been formed. Period.[15]

Negotiation, Mediation, Arbitration

Most pastors strive to grow spiritually and to encourage spiritual
growth in their congregations. But let's face it: the very nature of
church life itself is to minister to people who are at very different
points along the road in their spiritual journey. Even when churches
have exceptional discipleship programs available, only a limited
number of people take full advantage of all that is offered.

One of the most severe testings for any of us is found in
church conflict. The publication of so many books on this subject
testifies to our individual and corporate failures in responding to
conflict in a healthy way. Paul writes to the churches of Galatia,
"Brothers and sisters, if someone is caught in a sin, you who live by
the Spirit should restore that person gently. But watch yourselves,
or you also may be tempted" (6:1 NIV). Christians are called to

patiently assist those who are struggling in all areas of life, including church conflict.

Although non-Christian conflict resolution practitioners seldom acknowledge it, negotiation, mediation, and arbitration are all biblical models. Matthew 18:15–17 presents a clear progression of how to resolve interpersonal conflict. First is negotiation: "If your brother sins against you, go and tell him his fault, between you and him alone. If he listens to you, you have gained your brother." Second is mediation: "But if he does not listen, take one or two others along with you, that every charge may be established by the evidence of two or three witnesses." Third is arbitration: "If he refuses to listen to them, tell it to the church. And if he refuses to listen even to the church, let him be to you as a Gentile and a tax collector." Some have thought this last statement implies total rejection of an unrepentant person. However, it more likely means that we are to consider the person as unchristian and therefore treat him or her as an object of evangelism as we would anyone else outside the faith.[16]

Following Matthew 18 as a template for interpersonal conflict resolution is rare. From social media to politics to the workplace, talking negatively about a person who is not present is an all-too-common practice and deemed culturally acceptable.

One church had a deep-rooted history of gossip and slander. For decades, this sinful conduct was tolerated and even modeled by church leaders. When an interim pastor addressed the problem during a Sunday morning worship service, you could have heard a pin drop. He challenged the congregation when disagreements arose to practice Matthew 18 principles by confronting fellow parishioners one on one before involving any other parties in the conversation. He further admonished them to be intolerant of anyone who violated these principles by not entertaining gossip and instead redirecting offenders to speak with the person gently and privately with whom they were having a problem.

The congregation accepted the challenge. Over the next few months, the culture of gossip and conflict greatly diminished. Those who continued to gossip became visible to all and either lost their influence and credibility or left the church. Those few who stayed but continued to gossip were then subject to church discipline.

When a congregation becomes proficient at one-on-one confrontation (negotiation), the first step in Matthew 18, the next step is to equip several key leaders to serve as mediators and coaches within the congregation. Our next chapter looks at how to develop and practice these skills and processes.

Chapter 8

Interpersonal Conflict Part Two: Mediation

When Cephas came to Antioch, I opposed him to his face, because he stood condemned. For before certain men came from James, he was eating with the Gentiles; but when they came he drew back and separated himself, fearing the circumcision party. And the rest of the Jews acted hypocritically along with him, so that even Barnabas was led astray by their hypocrisy.
—Galatians 2:11–13

David said to Abigail: "Blessed is the LORD God of Israel, who sent you this day to meet me! And blessed is your advice and blessed are you, because you have kept me this day from coming to bloodshed and from avenging myself with my own hand."

—1 Samuel 25:32–33 NKJV

Mediation: Introducing the Process[17]

We began the last chapter with a brief account of two church staff members, Garry and Daniel, who were having difficulty working together. In this chapter we illustrate how a neutral third party can serve as a mediator to help identify and resolve the root causes of a dispute. Jack Burris is a Christian mediator from a nearby church who was recommended by a neighboring minister and invited to assist in improving the contentious relationship between these two pastors. Neither Garry nor Daniel had met Jack before then.

The mediation session

"Garry and Daniel, I commend you for allowing me to serve as your mediator today," Jack began. He briefly described his work as a mediator with the local school district, where he'd had fifteen years of experience. In addition, he had been a Christian for many years and frequently assisted people in his own church when mediation was needed. "Today and during any future meetings we might have," he assured the men, "you will be provided an opportunity to discuss your concerns to gain a better understanding of each other and to improve your working relationship. My role will be to help you identify issues, communicate clearly, and develop a plan to serve your church together more effectively."

Jack went on to explain that mediation[18] was a voluntary process. As the mediator, he did not have any authority and would not attempt to make any decisions for the parties involved. Instead, his role would be to guide the process to help facilitate their discussions while seeking to keep the process productive and on track. Any agreements can be formal or informal and, if desired, Jack would record any decisions made for future reference.

Jack explained further, "I will try to remain as impartial and objective as possible. I don't have any agenda other than attempting to help you find the best solutions possible. If at any time you feel I am taking sides, don't hesitate to stop the process so we can resolve your concerns. If we can't satisfactorily do that, you can end the mediation and find another mediator to help you."

Mediation is simply a structured approach to resolving interpersonal conflict. An objective third party can often help people who are stuck in conflict break an unhealthy spiral of negative communication patterns and forge a more constructive path forward. Mediation skills can be learned and applied by anyone willing to study and practice these techniques. As mentioned in the last chapter, mediation correlates to the second step in the conflict resolution process outlined in Matthew 18. The techniques themselves are a reflection of biblical communication principles put into action in a practical way. More details about this process and the biblical principles involved will be addressed in Section Three of this book. For now, we will see how mediation helped Garry and Daniel in their desire to break out of their dysfunctional working relationship.

Telling our stories

Jack continued, "A good place to begin is to invite each of you to explain the situation and issues that bring you to mediation today. But before we begin, would it be okay for me to offer a prayer for our time together?" Both men nodded. "Dear Father, thank You for this opportunity to work together for the kingdom. We need Your help today. Please guide our thoughts and words in a manner pleasing to You and in a way that brings unity and blessing. In Jesus' name I pray. Amen."

Then Jack explained what was next. "Each of you will have an opportunity to present your side of the story uninterrupted. You have a pen and pad in front of you. While listening to each other's presentations, you will most likely feel the need to interrupt and make corrections. When this happens, please simply write down any questions and concerns that you have so they can be addressed at the end of each presentation. I assure you that you will have good opportunity to do so."

Jack said he might ask some clarifying questions to make sure that sufficient information was shared to give full understanding. Once both Garry and Daniel were satisfied they had been heard and understood, the three would work to identify both the issues and the underlying interests they each feel needed to be addressed. When those were agreed on, "we'll brainstorm to find the best solutions. If at any time, either of you wish to leave the joint meeting to talk with me privately, you may do so," he told them. "Private sessions, called caucuses, are a normal part of the process. I too might ask for a private meeting with one or both of you. These caucuses, if needed, will provide an opportunity to discuss options and concerns and to handle strong emotions, and so on."

Jack assured Garry and Daniel that anything revealed in the mediation or caucus session(s) was confidential and would not be discussed with anyone not involved in the dispute unless they both gave him permission to do so.[19]

He then asked for the privilege of being able to talk with one or more of his mediation colleagues to better assist them in finding resolution. When doing so, he explained he would not reveal any personally identifying information or disclose their names but simply talk about issues and possible solutions.

"We have scheduled two hours for our session today. This may be enough time to reach a good solution. If not, we'll schedule another session as soon as practical as long as you both find this process helpful," Jack added. "At this point, I recommend some procedural guidelines found useful in negotiations. I invite you to establish some basic ground rules or guidelines to help the process run smoothly. I've already mentioned the need for you to speak without interruptions. Can we agree this is a reasonable guideline for these sessions?"

Daniel and Garry both nodded, and Jack wrote NO INTER-RUPTING WHILE ANOTHER IS SPEAKING on the whiteboard. Jack asked, "What other guidelines do you think will be helpful during this discussion today?"

Daniel suggested, "It will be good if we agree to remain respectful to each other."

Jack wrote MAINTAIN MUTUAL RESPECT. "Does this capture what you have in mind? Daniel, can you give an example?"

Daniel said, "Yes, I think we should show respect by not raising our voices and remaining calm . . . controlling our emotions," he added.

The process continued until both pastors were satisfied the needed behavioral guidelines were adequate for their discussion. Then Jack said, "Sometimes in important discussions like these, emotions can get heated, and when this happens, reminders may be needed to honor the ground rules you have laid out. How many times should we allow a violation before a consequence should ensue, and what consequence should it be?"

Garry replied with a slight smile, "Three strikes and you're out!" Both men laughed but agreed three violations should force a time-out until strong feelings could cool down and they were ready with a fresh commitment to continue. Jack asked for any questions before beginning opening statements. After a few questions about scheduling breaks, both pastors indicated they were ready to begin.

"Who would like to go first?" Jack asked.

"I would if it's okay with Daniel," Garry said.

Daniel agreed.

"I appreciate Daniel's ministry here, but it's been a bumpy ride from the beginning," Garry began. "I am the senior pastor and Daniel is my assistant. I have certain expectations of how things should be done and to be honest, Daniel seems like he really doesn't want to do things my way. It is one thing to disagree; it is another to be insubordinate!" Daniel started to say something but bit his tongue. Instead he began to write on the pad in front of him.

Jack interjected, "Can you give an example?"

Garry answered, "For one thing, I need to see a detailed agenda and approve it before any meetings that Daniel has planned take place. He knows what I want, but he refuses to do it!"

Daniel was writing furiously on his notepad.

"I also want him to keep a clear calendar of events I can access 24/7/365," Garry added. Garry continued to name item after item on his list of expectations and insisted Daniel was failing miserably to comply. After twenty minutes, Garry paused, and Jack asked if he had anything else to add.

"Those are the main things," Garry concluded. Jack then read the list back to them to make sure he had a full understanding.

After a few reiterations but no new information, Jack turned to Daniel and said, "Now it's your turn. Do you want to ask Garry for clarification or move directly to your side of the story?"

Daniel replied, "We've been over these issues so many times already that I would like to just tell my side."

Jack nodded for him to begin.

"Garry, I love and respect you and have never intentionally been insubordinate to you."

Garry began to interrupt, but Jack silently pointed to the guidelines on the whiteboard. Garry pulled back and said, "I forgot, sorry. I'll try not to do that again."

Daniel continued, "I always provide you with an outline of the agendas I'm planning for my meetings. You have access to my electronic calendar anytime you want. I don't know why you're continuously upset." Daniel went through Garry's list item by item, explaining how he had complied at every point.

When Daniel indicated that he had nothing further to add, Jack turned back to Garry and invited his response.

"You said that you always provide me with an agenda for your meetings—hardly! You jot down a few bullet points that have no meaning to me. I want more information. I need details to understand what's going on around here!" Garry's face was getting red, and his voice was getting louder.

Jack pointed to the ground rule MAINTAIN MUTUAL RESPECT, and Garry lowered his voice. As he continued to walk through his notes, it became clear that these two men were not at all on the same page. There seemed to be some level of disagreement on almost every point.

While they continued telling their stories, Jack wrote a list of issues on the board. The list was long. Jack then asked, "Do either of you have any concerns not covered somewhere in this list of issues?"

Both men stared intently at the board, comparing their handwritten notes to the list before them. After a few pointed questions to make sure the descriptors on the board were complete, both seemed satisfied their concerns were noted.

Working toward solutions

With the mediator's help, Garry and Daniel began to work their way through the list of issues Jack posted on the board. After prioritizing concerns, the first three issues are listed below as examples. The wording to describe each problem was discussed and reframed[20] by Jack to help understand the issues as substantive rather than personal. This helped both men calm their emotions by separating content issues from relational ones.

ISSUE	GARRY'S PERCEPTION	DANIEL'S PERCEPTION
Meeting Agendas	Detailed Content Missing	Outlines Sufficient
Daniel's Calendar	Daniel's Time Mgmt. Too Unstructured	Garry's Expectations Unreasonable
Philosophy of Ministry	Task Oriented	People Oriented

"Garry, how much detail do you need from Daniel in his meeting agendas?" Jack asked.

"More than I'm getting!" Garry snapped back.

"Do you have a sample agenda you could give Daniel to help him create the level of detail that you require?" Jack asked.

"I suppose," Garry replied.

"Can you help Daniel understand why this amount of detail is so important to you?" Jack asked.

"Even though these are Daniel's meetings, as senior pastor, ultimately I am responsible for what happens in this church. It's embarrassing for me when I get blindsided by someone asking questions I can't answer or I'm hearing things for the first time from a church member. They expect me to know what's going on in all the ministries of this church. This is especially true with the youth ministry activities," Garry explained.

"I didn't realize how you felt," Daniel replied. "I just thought you didn't trust me."

"I do *trust* you, Daniel; I just need to be able to answer people's questions and to have enough information to feel secure in my responsibilities as the senior pastor." Garry was speaking more calmly now.

Their two hours were up, and Jack asked if they would like to meet together again to continue their discussion. They both agreed. Jack had preassigned them spiritual gift inventories to complete. "Please bring your results to our next session, and we'll review the results together," he directed.

When they met for their next session a week later, Garry had already provided samples of his meeting agendas for Daniel to review. After a few clarifying questions, Daniel agreed to use Garry's samples as a template for future meetings. As Jack walked them through a discussion of each item on the list, they were able to gain understanding of their differing ministry styles and to come to agreements on how to meet each other's expectations. A review of the gift inventory helped both men appreciate each other's strengths and see how each one's gifts complemented the other's weaknesses.

The final task was to lay out a strategy together for any future disagreements. The mediation appeared to be a success, and both men agreed that next time they didn't think that they would need any help resolving their issues. But they did agree to return to mediation if they encountered conflicts in the future that they could not resolve themselves.

The next topic we tackle is intrapersonal conflict, i.e., those struggles that lie within us. These can be as significant as any other root causes we seek to identify and resolve and just as critical to church harmony!

Chapter 9

Personal (Inner) Conflict

Samuel said, "What have you done?" Saul said, "When I saw that the people were scattered from me, and that you did not come within the days appointed, and that the Philistines gathered together at Michmash, then I said, 'The Philistines will now come down on me at Gilgal, and I have not made supplication to the Lord.' Therefore, I felt compelled, and offered a burnt offering."
—1 Samuel 13:11–12 NKJV

That person must not suppose that he will receive anything from the Lord; he is a double-minded man, unstable in all his ways.
— James 1:7–8

Spiritual and Ethical Issues

FIRST CITY CHURCH: THE CASE OF THE MISSING FUNDS

"I'm ready to file a lawsuit," Seth announced. The other members of the youth ministry board sat silently, trying to absorb what they had just heard. "We're working too hard to reach these kids to have our part of the budget stolen!" he added.

Jill finally spoke up. "Seth, we don't know that anyone is actually stealing our funds, do we?"

"The numbers just don't add up!" Seth replied with considerable anger in his voice. "I've been asking questions long enough and not getting any answers. I think it's time we get to the bottom of this or I'm calling a lawyer."

Seth and his wife, Sally, had poured out their hearts and

souls—not to mention their time, hard work, and money—in a effort to reach the inner-city youth from this poor, violent neighborhood. The old three-story church building had boarded up the top floor decades ago as church attendance and finances steadily declined.

But now, thanks to Seth, Sally, and a handful of dedicated volunteers, the third floor was reclaimed, and an effective outreach ministry was taking off. True, they had had to install a metal detector at the door, but the word was out, and an increasing number of neighborhood kids were showing up every week. So far, a gymnasium, a theater, and a computer lab were available, with even more good things on the drawing board! But the excitement was turning to frustration for Seth because the money coming in for youth ministry never seemed to make it to the top-floor project. The explanations always seemed sincere but never fully convincing. The money was going somewhere, but it wasn't to the outreach ministry of First City Church!

This downtown congregation had become a revolving door for pastors and currently they didn't have one. The denomination was sending green candidates fresh out of seminary because no one else was willing to come. With a weekly rotation of pulpit supply, leadership was falling to a deeply divided board, and most ministry positions were being filled with anyone they could rope into filling an empty slot. The treasurer and financial secretary seemed surprised when the district superintendent of the denomination called a meeting to investigate Seth's continuing complaints.

The people seated around the table this Saturday morning included the chairs of all the church's committees, its two financial officers, and Rusty Harper, the denominational official who had been invited due to the serious nature of the issue. Seth and Sally were also present since their complaints prompted this meeting with the superintendent. Bob Jenkins was also present even though he didn't hold any official position within the church. He was a revered, longtime member, and the single largest contributor to the congregation. He was at the meeting because of his historical knowledge of church operations. Rusty Harper called the meeting to order and opened with a brief prayer.

"Thank you for inviting me here today. I appreciate opportunities to serve the churches in my district," he began. He continued, "First City Church has been here longer than any of us and has a great legacy in our area. I understand there are questions about the budget and how funds are allocated and spent, is that correct?" Those present indicated agreement. Rusty went on. "I have asked each of you to bring relevant records from your various ministries including minutes from the last six months of operation," he explained. "If we need additional information going back further than six months, let's try to get those documents here as quickly as possible. Let's begin by looking at the annual budget as approved."

As copies of the budget were distributed and explained by the treasurer, Rusty asked for each committee chair to examine their minutes for spending decisions as aligned with the planned budget categories. Each time, Nancy, the financial secretary, attempted to find the record for each expenditure and provide the date and records used for these purchases or payments.

It quickly became apparent that Nancy was finding expenditures with no authorizing decisions recorded in the minutes. At first, the types of unauthorized purchases that were identified seemed random. When several were isolated and questions were raised about which ministry or project the purchases were for, Bob Jenkins became visibly uncomfortable. Suddenly, he interrupted the meeting by standing up and stating that he needed to leave to take care of some personal business.

Rusty Harper expressed disappointment and asked him to stay until the issues could be resolved. However, Bob insisted his business couldn't wait and promptly gathered his things and departed. Although clearly surprised by Bob's unexpected departure, the group returned to their discussion of unauthorized expenditures.

Luis Alvarez, trustee board chair, spoke next. "These expenditures all seem to be related to Bob's community educational project." Luis's words seemed to hang in the air.

Finally, Carolyn Robinson, a longtime church member and missions committee chair, said, "It's no secret that Bob is a generous and faithful contributor to this church."

"I knew these numbers weren't adding up, and I wondered about Bob," Seth confessed. "But I think the world of him, and I really don't want to cause him any trouble." He added, "Why wouldn't he just give the money directly to his charity instead of passing it through the church?"

"I may know the answer to that question," Luis replied. "One of the foundations that Bob created is structured to give 100 percent of their receipts directly to our church. Maybe he feels like this is his money to direct wherever he wants."

Rusty Harper interrupted the dialogue. "If this is what Bob is doing, it's unacceptable, regardless of his motives. I know that many people in this church love this man and don't want to hurt him, but the church needs to decide how to deal with his actions and take care of this as quickly as possible."

Working together, those members who knew Bob best met privately with him and advised him of the church's concerns. He agreed to apologize to the members at a specially called meeting, and rectify the financial situation to the board's satisfaction. He did so and found ready forgiveness. Financial policies and procedures were also tightened to prevent similar problems from occurring in the future.

Personal or intrapersonal conflict does not require that the individual feel conflicted within him or herself. The significance here is to recognize that some church conflicts can have their origins *within an individual* rather than in disagreements between people or groups, or from organizational deficits. In these cases, the solution requires diagnosing and resolving the conflict by responding to the root cause.

Obviously, as is true in this case, finding the root cause also helps to identify other secondary issues or deficits that also need resolving (e.g., poor accounting and/or auditing practices). Stress and conflict no doubt occurred within and between groups and individuals because of the financial problems and pressures created. However, in this case, underneath it all were the unethical choices and actions of one person who needed to be identified and confronted. In other intrapersonal cases, the issues might be biological, psychological, theological, or spiritual, or some combination of all of these. Regardless, resolving the root cause(s) is key to finding sustainable solutions.

Psychological Issues

ELM AND CHASE STREET CHURCH:
THE CASE OF THE MISSING LEADER

"Fred's not here again, and I don't think he's coming," Elizabeth said with disappointment in her voice. The executive board members sitting around the table seemed to sigh in unison.

"How does he expect us to get anything done around here?" Micah asked rhetorically.

"Not long ago a team of wild horses couldn't have kept him away. This is his project, and he seemed keen to get things moving," C. J. added. "But lately, all he does is become agitated and throw cold water on every idea we come up with."

"We agreed not to move forward without unanimous approval,

and this really can't happen without the chairman's vote!" Elizabeth said, her frustration apparent.

"I think that we should call Pastor Smithson and let him know no decision is coming tonight," C. J. said.

Elm and Chase Street Church moved cautiously toward their new building program. Their building was filled to capacity and had been for years, a good problem to have. Holding multiple services solved the situation for a while but now even parking had become a major difficulty. When a thirty-acre parcel of land had been donated a year ago by a local rancher, it seemed like the sign everyone was hoping for.

Fred Jamison, a small business owner, was the biggest cheerleader for building a new church. But something was happening to Fred. In recent months he seemed to vacillate between his usual upbeat and exuberant self to becoming a depressed and agitated contrarian. That is, when he showed up at all. The momentum that had been building for months in the congregation was starting to wane, and the timing couldn't have been worse. Fred's once strong and inspiring leadership was instead becoming a roller-coaster ride of mixed messages, and had everyone worried and confused.

The day after the meeting, Pastor Jeb Smithson called Fred to set up a meeting that afternoon if possible, and Fred agreed. Soon Fred was sitting on a chair in front of the pastor's desk, his eyes not quite meeting Jeb's. "Fred, thanks for making time to meet with me," Pastor Smithson said in a welcoming tone, and he extended his hand warmly.

"Sure," Fred said a bit nervously.

"First, I want to thank you for all you're doing to support our building project. Your enthusiastic leadership on the board and your inspiring words to the congregation are amazing," Jeb assured him. "I have no doubt your presence and influence have made an enormous difference."

"Thanks," Fred replied without looking up.

"I am worried about you, however, Fred. Is everything okay? C. J. called me last night and expressed concern that you weren't at the board meeting. He said that everyone was set to vote on the next phase of the project but couldn't move forward because your absence prevented a unanimous vote. What happened?"

"I'm sorry, Pastor. I've not been myself lately," Fred replied, still not meeting Jeb's eyes.

"What are you not telling me?" Jeb asked gently.

Fred sat despondently without speaking for nearly a full minute. "I've got a problem that I haven't told anyone about," he said finally. "About six months ago, I was diagnosed with bipolar disorder. They put me on medication, but I've stopped taking it."

"Fred, I am so sorry to hear that you're facing this challenge. I can only imagine how difficult this must be. How can I help?" Jeb said quietly. He left his desk and put his hand on Fred's shoulder.

"I don't think there is anything anyone can do. I thought the medication was the answer, but the side effects are awful. When I take the medicine, I feel dead inside. And when I don't take it, I can't sleep. I haven't slept for days; that's why I missed the meeting last night. I'm so sorry—I know I should have been there," Fred told him.

The pastor pulled a chair alongside of Fred's and sat quietly for a few moments before he said, "Fred, the most important thing now is to make sure you get the help you need. You have a family to take care of. How's Luci handling all this? Is there anything we can do to help?"

"We're both frustrated, Luci and I; even afraid."

That evening Pastor Jeb made a home visit and encouraged Fred and Luci to seek out a second opinion. Fred found a different doctor who worked with him and was able to guide him to successfully manage his illness. Fred soon met with the board to explain his circumstances. They were encouraging and supportive during his treatment and recovery. It took several months, but Fred was then able to reengage, and Elm and Chase successfully moved ahead and eventually completed their building program. Fred's personal struggle needed to be identified and resolved before everything could get back on track.

Intrapersonal issues, whether they are spiritual, physical, or emotional can be serious obstacles, and identifying and resolving root causes can be challenging. However, as in all other categories of conflict, they can provide significant opportunities for change and growth, both for individuals and for organizations.

Chapter 10

Forgiveness

Be kind to one another, tenderhearted,
forgiving one another, as God in Christ forgave you.
—Ephesians 4:32

Unforgiveness is the poison we drink hoping others will die.
—Marianne Williamson

"I will never forgive you, Caleb! You have humiliated me in front of the whole church!"

Caleb Hart was shocked by Terry's response. In the business meeting, Pastor Terry Hathaway had proposed the purchase of land adjacent to the church property, to build a new sanctuary.

Caleb had become very enthusiastic about the preaching and the outreach ministries of Cloverfield Fellowship, and now, as a new member, had just attended his first business meeting of the church. He had asked several questions regarding finances during the meeting to better understand the rationale and feasibility of such a purchase. But he was blindsided by the pastor's strong words as these two men walked to the parking lot.

"Pastor, I can see you are very upset," Caleb replied softly. "Was it my questions during the meeting that upset you?"

Pastor Terry's face was red and his voice trembled as he replied with cutting sarcasm. "What do you think? You made me look like a fool in there!"

"Pastor, I never meant to embarrass you. Did you feel like I was challenging your proposal, is that why you are angry?" Caleb again inquired, quietly.

Pastor Terry stopped walking and looked Caleb in the eye. "Of course, you were challenging me, and in front of the whole church! How did you think that would make me feel?"

"I am so sorry. I hope you can forgive me," Caleb replied. Both men walked to their cars in silence. "Can we talk more about this tomorrow?" Caleb asked, but there was no reply.

At one time or another, we've all had experiences like this one. Forgiveness does not come naturally.

Any discussion of conflict resolution is incomplete without addressing forgiveness. Although this book's primary focus is on how to analyze and resolve organizational conflict, forgiveness is vital to healing in all broken relationships. Although unforgiveness usually surfaces first in interpersonal disagreement, personal offenses take place in all levels of conflict. Regardless of our success in accurately analyzing and structuring interventions to address organizational disputes, unless people forgive one another, any seeming successes will be short-lived.

A Theology of Forgiveness

Should we forgive someone who has sinned against us, who is unrepentant, and/or who continues to sin against us? This is the same question Peter asked Jesus:

> Peter came to Him and said, "Lord, how often shall my brother sin against me, and I forgive him? Up to seven times?" Jesus said to him, "I do not say to you, up to seven times, but up to seventy times seven." (Matt. 18:21–22 NKJV)

Peter no doubt thought that he was being generous because the Jewish tradition stipulated an obligation of only forgiving a person up to three times.[21] Jesus wasn't simply increasing the number to 490 (some versions render this "seventy-seven").

Instead, the biblical standard is for us to forgive others in the same limitless way in which God forgives us (Eph. 4:32). In Luke 17:4, Jesus adds that we are to forgive even if someone sins against us seven times in the same day! Some offenses can be overlooked (Prov. 19:11), while others should not (Matt. 18:15). But forgiveness should be a constant in all our relationships.

Forgiveness and reconciliation, however, are two different things. Confusing them can lead to our holding a grudge and harboring resentment unless or until the offending party repents and apologizes. Reconciliation is wonderful, but it's not always possible, because it depends on a godly response from both parties (Rom. 12:18). Forgiveness, however, depends only on us.[22] We can forgive even if the offending party is unresponsive. Once we forgive, we are freed from the burden of the offense(s), and the other person is left to decide about his or her own spiritual choices and consequences.

Forgiving does not mean we no longer believe a wrong was committed. Forgiveness doesn't change the facts, only our spiritual disposition toward those facts. One definition of forgiveness is "choosing to no longer hold the offense against a person." It is also important to understand that to forgive does not mean that we must immediately trust the other person. Trust must be earned. In many cases, the injured party is wise to be cautious and protect themselves from further injury if or until trust can be reestablished.

Moving toward forgiveness and reconciliation

Scripture teaches that whether we are the offending party or the party feeling offended, we have the mandate to initiate forgiveness and reconciliation:

> "If your brother sins against you, go and tell him his fault, between you and him alone." (Matt. 18:15)

If you are offering your gift at the altar and there remember that
your brother has something against you, leave your gift there before
the altar and go. First be reconciled to your brother, and then come
and offer your gift. (Matt. 5:23–24)

God evidently values interpersonal reconciliation as a necessary prerequisite to our own personal worship!

I once witnessed a beautiful example of this reconciliation process during a service at a church I was visiting. The congregation
was large, and the ushers were well trained and moved with near
military precision in distributing the elements of Communion. I
saw one usher break formation and walk over to whisper something
in the ear of a fellow usher. These two men spoke quietly to each
other and then appeared to pray together. It all happened quickly,
and they returned to their duties and the service continued.

What I suspected happened was later confirmed by a member
of the congregation. One of these ushers was convicted as the
pastor invited the congregation to prepare their hearts for the
Lord's Supper about an unresolved issue with his fellow usher. He
felt compelled to ask forgiveness before he could take Communion. He asked and received forgiveness and the two prayed briefly
together. While some may think these actions should have waited
until after the Communion service, I believe it is a perfect illustration of the urgency and primacy of the immediate obedience God
emphasizes in Matthew chapter 5.

Equipping ourselves to forgive

Since forgiveness does not come naturally to any of us, we
must prepare ourselves to obey. The Scripture shows us how.
First, we must understand the old nature. Jeremiah 17:9 reads,
"The heart is deceitful above all things, *and desperately sick; who can
understand it?*"

I once heard someone say, "The problem with self-deceit is that we don't know we've been deceived." If forgiveness is not natural, it must be supernatural. What is natural is the desire for revenge and retaliation. First Corinthians 2:14 reminds us, "The natural person does not accept the things of the Spirit of God, for they are folly to him, and he is not able to understand them because they are spiritually discerned."

If we are not to be conformed to this world but rather transformed by the Spirit (Rom. 12:2), this is a great time to reflect on our attitudes and perspectives regarding forgiveness and reconciliation. Second Corinthians 5:17 tells us where this starts: "Therefore, if anyone is in Christ, he is a new creation. The old has passed away; behold, the new has come." Romans 12:21 commands us, "Do not be overcome by evil, but overcome evil with good." So the first step toward becoming a forgiving person is to think biblically about it.

The next step is to *act* biblically toward others when we are offended or when we are the offender. Ken Sande in his book *The Peacemaker* offers simple alliteration devices and acrostics to remember biblical principles to better navigate these emotionally challenging waters.[23] As mentioned in chapter 3 of this book, training in godliness requires us to replace old habits with new ones. Just reading about these principles is not enough; they must be practiced until they become second nature. Otherwise, our old nature will remain our default reaction when conflicts emerge.

Dr. Everett Worthington, a Christian psychologist specializing in the study of forgiveness, suggests there are two types of forgiveness: *decisional forgiveness* and *emotional forgiveness*. He contends that deciding to forgive can be done more easily than overcoming our negative emotions and experiencing the peace God gives, but both parts are crucial to forgiving. He offers a five-step model and resources to help people work through both types. These follow the acronym REACH:

1. **R**ecall the Hurt
2. **E**mpathize with the One Who Hurt You
3. Give an **A**ltruistic Gift of Forgiveness
4. **C**ommit to the Forgiveness You Experienced
5. **H**old on to Forgiveness and Become a More Forgiving Person[24]

Listening and Speaking

Effective listening

In James 1:19, we're reminded to be "quick to hear, slow to speak, slow to anger." Listening well is difficult. Here again, our old nature works powerfully against us. It is normal and natural to focus on our own self-interests. Philippians 2:3, however, admonishes us to "do nothing from selfish ambition or conceit, but in humility count others more significant than yourselves." Good listening includes the ability to set aside our self-protective reactions and thoughts and to instead focus on the concerns of the other person. From a practical standpoint, developing such skills as asking, mirroring, and paraphrasing can help create safety and show interest.[25]

Meaningful conversation and genuine apology

Proverbs tells us that "a soft answer turns away wrath, but a harsh word stirs up anger" (15:1) and "a word fitly spoken is like apples of gold in a setting of silver " (25:11). Wisdom requires our words to be carefully chosen if we hope to bring about positive outcomes in times of conflict.

Together, listening and conversation skills can be a powerful combination in improving communication in difficult circumstances. It is also vital to recognize the importance of apology when we have hurt another person. There are so many ways to apologize badly. Usually, watching or reading the apologies of politicians is an excellent way to learn how *not* to apologize! Many of these statements were crafted by attorneys to avoid liability or any confession of guilt (true acceptance of responsibility) and projecting the problem back onto the person feeling offended.

One common example we often hear is, "If anyone felt offended, I am truly sorry." Although this may sound like a real apology, the word "if" deflects the responsibility onto the person(s) feeling offended. The implication is that the offended party (or parties) may be at fault for misunderstanding or being overly sensitive. Sincerity and transparency are vital (and often lacking), but being genuinely sorry is usually not enough. The words that are used can either negate or enhance the effectiveness of an apology.

Gary Chapman and Jennifer Thomas offer an interesting approach to the differing needs people have in order to benefit from an apology. Here are differences in the wording of five apology statements that their research has shown to be effective in varying contexts with differing personalities:[26]

1. "I'm sorry." (expressing regret)
2. "I was wrong." (accepting responsibility)
3. "What can I do to make it right?" (making restitution)
4. "I'll try not to do that again." (genuinely repenting)
5. "Will you please forgive me?" (requesting forgiveness)

This research indicates that different people need to hear different words to experience an apology in a meaningful way. Their recommendation is that we use them all when we don't know which "language of apology" a person needs to hear.

Hebrews 12:15–17 reminds us that the spiritual condition of our heart affects not only us but also all those around us:

Work at getting along with each other and with God. Otherwise

you'll never get so much as a glimpse of God. Make sure no one gets
left out of God's generosity. Keep a sharp eye out for weeds of bitter
discontent. A thistle or two gone to seed can ruin a whole garden
in no time. Watch out for the Esau syndrome: trading away God's
lifelong gift in order to satisfy a short-term appetite. You well know
how Esau later regretted that impulsive act and wanted God's blessing—but by then it was too late, tears or no tears. (MSG)

Caleb Hart and Pastor Hathaway eventually talked through the
painful episode mentioned at the beginning of this chapter. When
they were able to calm down, they both realized that their relationship was more important to God, to the church, and to each other
than being right or worrying about damaged pride. Terry sincerely
listened to Caleb's heart and understood the good motives behind
his questions. Caleb realized how he might have approached things
differently without embarrassing Pastor Hathaway publicly. Today
they are good friends and enjoy serving together in the business of
the church. Learning to forgive is a critical part of resolving conflict
biblically.

Chapter 11

Conflict Styles, Spiritual Gifts, and Skill Development

*The world cannot hate you, but it hates me because I testify
about it that its works are evil. You go up to the feast. I am
not going up to this feast, for my time has not yet fully come.*
—John 7:7–8

*Making a whip of cords, he drove them all out of the temple,
with the sheep and oxen. And he poured out the coins of
the money-changers and overturned their tables.*
—John 2:15

Conflict Styles

"If you've got something to say to me, just say it!" an exasperated
Frank said.

"It's nothing, really. I'm sorry I mentioned anything," Aaron
replied.

Aaron is twenty years younger than Frank and a self-confessed
introvert. Frank manages an auto parts store and is quick to take
the lead on any project to which he is assigned. Both men serve
on the church trustee board and have had some trouble working
together. Their communication styles are clearly different, which
affects how they deal with the inevitable conflicts that come along.

Much has been written about the differences that exist between people in how they respond to conflict. One classic model

presents five different conflict styles: Collaborating, Competing, Accommodating, Avoiding, and Compromising.[27] A number of adaptations and variations of this model have been published in recent years. Most conflict style assessment tools are designed to measure a person's dominant manner of responding to disagreement and conflict, and then ranking their remaining styles from second down to last. The stated purpose generally is to help individuals become more self-aware of their predominant conflict style and learn to recognize and use the other styles through intentional practice. The Scriptures seem to confirm the need to respond to situational conflicts differently and illustrate these differences in how biblical characters reacted to the conflicted circumstances that they encountered.

Another way to conceptualize these differences is to view them in terms of individual personalities and spiritual gifting characteristics. The preeminent example for us to emulate, of course, is found in the life of Jesus. There were times when Jesus avoided conflict and other times when He confronted disputes head-on. It is obvious from His life, since He always handled circumstances and people perfectly, that differing situations call for different responses and strategies.

Jesus often confronted the religious leaders of His day with surprising candor. For example, He called out the Pharisees publicly as hypocrites and vipers. At other times, He clearly postponed conflict with these same leaders, stating His time had not fully come. He was sometimes gentle when confronting sinners, as with the woman caught in adultery, and aggressive with others as when He openly rebuked the Pharisees and when He purged the temple of money-changers.

Sometimes conflict avoidance reveals fearfulness and even cowardice. At other times it reflects godly discernment and wisdom. Both timing and the manner of confronting can be critical factors in demonstrating Christian love and discipline in bringing healthy dialogue and sustainable resolution.

Similarly, the apostle Paul demonstrated two different "conflict styles" when he reasoned with the Greek philosophers on Mars Hill (Acts 17) and later when he rebuked Peter in front of the brethren for his duplicitous actions before Jews and Gentiles (Gal. 2:11–14). Reflecting on Paul's communication style, one might conclude that he was generally bold and direct in his dealings with people, perhaps evidencing spiritual leadership gifts such as prophesy, administration, and admonition. Other biblical characters such as the apostle John and Barnabas seem to reflect softer gifts like mercy, compassion, and encouragement.

While the constellations of spiritual gifts and personality characteristics differ in each of us, as we submit to the Holy Spirit, He can and will guide and direct us to shape our responses to conflict regardless of our gift mix. Having said that, some people are better suited for conflict work than others, and selecting people to serve in conflict resolution ministries requires the same spiritual discernment and common sense as choosing people to serve in other roles (e.g., music, teaching, counseling, administration, and so on).

Spiritual Gifts

Spiritual gifts are divinely distributed and sovereignly purposed. They empower us supernaturally to fulfill our individual callings while at the same time motivating us to partner with others in a God-given interdependency that fulfills His corporate purposes for the church. A close friend and colleague said, "The gifts that we don't have are just as important as the gifts that we do have. They tell us with whom we need to partner."[28]

A believer who refuses to use the gifts of others restricts his or her ministry to the limitations of their own gift(s). It is only when we submit to God's design for the body of Christ that we can enjoy a holistic and well-rounded ministry utilizing all of God's gifts and not confining the ministry simply to our own. In Romans 12:3–8 Paul entreats us:

> By the grace given to me I say to everyone among you not to think of himself more highly than he ought to think, but to think with sober judgment, each according to the measure of faith that God has assigned. For as in one body we have many members, and the members do not all have the same function, so we, though many, are one body in Christ, and individually members one of another. Having gifts that differ according to the grace given to us, let us use them: if prophecy, in proportion to our faith; if service, in our serving; the one who teaches, in his teaching; the one who exhorts, in his exhortation; the one who contributes, in generosity; the one who leads, with zeal; the one who does acts of mercy, with cheerfulness.

Not to recognize the gifts of others is to think of ourselves more highly than we ought. Although we are responsible in every area of discipleship regardless of gifting (e.g., evangelism, giving, praying), it is equally important to allow God to orchestrate the gifts of the whole body. And although there is no gift of "peacemaking" per se, some gifts seem especially conducive to resolving conflict.

As noted above, Barnabas's gifts appear especially well-suited for peacemaking. His name means "son of consolation" or "son of encouragement" (Acts 4:36). In that passage, he demonstrates a heart of generosity and benevolence. In Acts 15, Barnabas and Paul have "a sharp disagreement" over whether or not to include John Mark in their next missionary journey (v. 39). John Mark had previously deserted Paul on a similar mission.

Barnabas was ready to give John Mark a second chance, but Paul refused. Barnabas and Paul parted ways and apparently never ministered together again. However, Paul later reaffirms his confidence in Barnabas (1 Cor. 9:6) and calls John Mark his valued colaborer (2 Tim. 4:11). Who was right and who was wrong? Scripture doesn't say. This incident may demonstrate that a mix of gifts in different people can be valuable in resolving complex conflicts in ministry. Barnabas's compassion for John Mark may have been exactly what was needed to encourage him to continue in the Way. And Paul's leadership gifts seem exactly what was needed to make the final decision to bring Silas on as a partner. Regardless, God redeemed these circumstances for good. Had Barnabas and Paul worked more collaboratively together, perhaps the same outcome could have been accomplished without the painful dissension and broken relationships.

Spiritual gifts and conflict resolution

Discover Your God-Given Gifts is one book that focuses on what its authors refer to as the "motivational gifts" and can serve here as an example of how spiritual gifts can be understood in relationship to conflict resolution aptitudes or proclivities.[29] The authors address the gifts listed in Romans 12:6–8: Perceiver (Prophesy), Server, Teacher, Exhorter, Giver, Administrator, and Compassion (Mercy). In part, their definitions of these gifts include the following brief descriptions along with a functional analogy as related to the body of Christ:

1. **Perceiver**: One who clearly perceives the will of God. Eye of the body (spiritual insight).
2. **Server**: "Doer" or one who loves to serve others. Hands of the body (hands-on helper).
3. **Teacher**: One who loves to research and communicate truth. Mind of the body (search Scripture to inform and equip).

4. **Exhorter**: One who loves to encourage others to live a victorious life. Mouth of the body (speak to encourage and console).

5. **Giver**: One who loves to give time, talent, energy, and means to benefit others. Arms of the body (provide strength and support).

6. **Administrator**: One who loves to organize, lead, or direct—facilitator or leader. Shoulders of the body (carry the load of leadership).

7. **Compassion**: One who shows mercy, love, and care to those in need. Heart of the body (love wholeheartedly).

The point here is not to rank these gifts as most or least helpful in resolving conflict but rather to illustrate how people with differing gifts and gift mixes can work together in multiple ways to help others solve their problems and reconcile their relationships. Consider, for example, the following contributions that people with these differing gifts (or combinations of gifts) could provide before, during, and after a mediation or facilitated problem-solving session:

1. **Perceiver**: One who clearly perceives the will of God. Eye of the body (spiritual insight). Often, when conflict occurs, there is a need for someone to confront sinful behaviors by speaking the truth in love. As painful as this can be, it takes a discerning person to recognize and deliver such a message biblically.

2. **Server**: "Doer" or one who loves to serve others. Hands of the body (hands-on helper). Servers are energized by completing tasks in many roles—such as administrative assistants and receptionists—and in manual projects, such as setting up tables and chairs, bringing refreshments,

making copies, running errands, and so on. Performing these types of services is not only necessary but can provide a great opportunity for using one's gifts while serving others in meaningful ways.

3. **Teacher**: One who loves to research and communicate truth. Mind of the body (search Scripture to inform and equip). Teachers can clarify biblical principles, teach methods and processes, research records, provide training, and so on. Without these tasks being done effectively, efforts to resolve conflict successfully will certainly fail.

4. **Exhorter**: One who loves to encourage others to live a victorious life. Mouth of the body (speak to encourage and console). Conflict is often emotionally and spiritually exhausting and is also very discouraging. Exhorters can help conflicted parties see the redemptive aspects of even the most painful experiences and circumstances.

5. **Giver**: One who loves to give time, talent, energy, and means to benefit others. Arms of the body (provide strength and support). Conflict resolution often takes a great deal of time and energy. Givers have the needed discernment, sacrificial attitudes, and resources to effectively help others, especially in times of great need.

6. **Administrator**: One who loves to organize, lead, or direct—facilitator or leader. Shoulders of the body (carry the load of leadership). Although much of what is needed for effective conflict resolution is collaborative in nature, leadership and decision-making are always important factors, especially when people are impatient, indecisive, and/or unrepentant.

7. **Compassion**: One who shows mercy, love, and care to those in need. Heart of the body (love others selflessly and wholeheartedly). We serve a merciful God, and we are all

in great need of mercy. Those who have the gift of compassion can often provide hope and help when things would otherwise seem completely hopeless.

Building skills to resolve conflict

All of us can become more skilled at peacemaking. Developing greater awareness of our own gifts, strengths, and weaknesses can help us be more sensitive to the feelings and sensitivities of others. David manifests an exceptional self-awareness in the psalms both through his relationship with God and in his ability to read and understand others.

Author and teacher Ken Sande divides our personal skills into a triad model of self-awareness, other-awareness, and God-awareness. He also offers practical counterparts to each of these components: self-engagement, other-engagement, and God-engagement.[30] He likens these attributes to the secular model of Emotional Intelligence (EI)[31] but with an added theological dimension. In his model, which he calls Relational Wisdom, he utilizes biblical references to illustrate all three dimensions and provides practical questions and exercises to help with personal application.

Theoretical and theological learning of concepts and principles is important to developing skills in conflict resolution, but engaging in actual practice of methods and strategies is also extremely helpful. Like many practical skills, these can only become fully effective when used in simulations or role-plays or in real-life situations.

Another ministry formerly led by Ken Sande and now by Brian Noble is called Peacemakers.[32] Peacemakers provides training and intervention services to individuals and churches. As previously noted, negotiation, mediation, and arbitration have their origins in biblical principles and methods. Most communities have opportunities available to receive training in these practice areas, especially in mediation.

Although many of these resources are secular in nature, the skills they teach are easily recognizable as scriptural and adaptable to biblical principles and models (e.g., process structure, communication techniques) and can be valuable to church leaders. A typical training framework consists of forty contact hours of teaching and role-play practicums in which individuals can gain experience in hands-on application of these skills. These resources are most frequently found in community service contexts such as mediation centers, community colleges, the Better Business Bureau, and local court training programs. A number of online training programs are also available.[33] However, face-to-face role-play exercises are vital in learning and using mediation skills effectively.

SECTION THREE

THE
WORKBOOK

Chapter 12

Preparing for the Challenge

Which of you, desiring to build a tower, does not first sit down and count the cost, whether he has enough to complete it?
—Luke 14:28

Tell him, "Let not him who straps on his armor boast himself as he who takes it off."
—1 Kings 20:11

Understanding the Principles

The first thing that has to change is our attitudes. Most people seem to hate conflict and avoid it at all costs, while a few people seem to actually enjoy it. It is the rare leader who can use disagreement and conflict to solve issues in a healthy manner. We're all different—raised by different parents, endowed with different gifts. But I think on this we can all agree: the guidance of Scripture supersedes all those differences. First Corinthians 10:31 reads, "So, whether you eat or drink, or whatever you do, do all to the glory of God." We can and should view conflict as an opportunity!

James chapter 1 reads:

James, a servant of God and of the Lord Jesus Christ, to the twelve tribes in the Dispersion: Greetings. Count it all joy, my brothers, when you meet trials of various kinds, for you know that the testing of your faith produces steadfastness. And let steadfastness have its full effect, that you may be perfect and complete, lacking in nothing. (vv. 1–4).

James, the Lord's brother, reveals a great deal in these brief verses about God's perspective on how his readers' attitudes should respond to difficult experiences. This provides great instruction for us as well. James writes he is "a servant of God and of the Lord Jesus Christ." First, notice James didn't always feel this way. John 7:5 states, "For not even his [Jesus'] brothers believed in him." James, who evidently didn't believe until after the resurrection, now refers to himself not as Jesus' half brother but as a servant of the Lord Jesus Christ. The significance of this becomes evident in his next words: "to the twelve tribes in the Dispersion." James can now fully identify with his audience because he is suffering with them. The trials and conflict his brothers and sisters are experiencing he knows too well.

These Jews are being persecuted on at least three levels. First, they are suffering because they are Jews. Second, they are suffering because they are Christians—persecuted both by the world and by their unconverted brethren. Third, they are suffering because they are strangers who have been scattered in the Dispersion. Some scholars believe many were even homeless.

James then writes, "Greetings. Count it all joy, my brothers, when you meet trials of various kinds." What kind of joy? All joy. Those words connote pure joy, unadulterated joy. In other words, complete joy from which nothing can be added or taken away! And to what kind of trials should they (we) respond with this absolute joy? The words translated "various kinds" signifies every kind of trial possible. In the Greek translation of the Old Testament (Septuagint), this is the same word used to describe Joseph's coat of many colors—multifaceted and reflecting light in every direction.[34]

What does this have to do with the theology of conflict?[37] It means when we face disagreement and conflict, we can know that our response can and should be with pure joy! Why? Because we "know that the testing of [our] faith produces steadfastness. And [we are to] let steadfastness have its full effect, that [we] may be perfect and complete, lacking in nothing."

Some compare letting "steadfastness have its full effect" to being placed in a frying pan, getting hotter and hotter. Every fiber of our being wants to jump out. But instead, we remain in the skillet until God perfects a work in our lives. "Perfect and complete, lacking in nothing" signifies spiritual growth until we reach full maturity. In other words, trials and tribulation—even church conflict—are good for us when we allow God to use such experiences redemptively in our lives!

Many other passages in Scripture teach these same principles. Consider Joseph's brothers, whose conflict and sin led to his slavery and imprisonment. When his brothers expressed fear of retaliation from Joseph, he stated, "Do not fear, for am I in the place of God? As for you, you meant evil against me, but God meant it for good, to bring it about that many people should be kept alive, as they are today" (Gen. 50:19–20). And we are all familiar with the passage teaching this principle in Romans 8:28: "We know that for those who love God all things work together for good, for those who are called according to his purpose." God uses even conflict for good!

Putting Your Knowledge to Work

In the exercises that follow, you'll have an opportunity to reflect on current or past situation(s) in which the principles you have learned can (or could have) been put to good use in achieving healthy outcomes. In selecting your case study, choose a conflict that is complex enough to include factors in all five levels of the model. For example, think of situations where there were both individuals and groups in disagreement and where organizational factors such as policies and procedures or theological or philosophical issues were present.

YOUR TURN . . .

EXERCISE

Think of a conflict in the past and how you felt about your circumstances at the time. Choose one you responded to poorly or one that had unhealthy dynamics and a disappointing outcome. How could the biblical principles referenced earlier in this chapter have potentially provided a more constructive approach?

_____

_____

_____

_____

_____

_____

_____

_____

_____

_____

(Use additional paper if needed)

Equipping your church

Thomas Barrington is the senior pastor of Riverdale Church. The church is not in crisis currently. But Thomas feels a responsibility to prepare his church for the inevitable conflicts that will come. Six church leaders are attending a daylong equipping retreat designed to help them develop a hands-on training curriculum in conflict resolution training.

After Jenny Brooks, the Christian education director, opened their time in prayer, Thomas began the retreat by saying, "The world is filled with conflict. From the beginning to the end, conflict is a part of reality and it always has been—starting in the garden of Eden. There won't be lasting peace until the Prince of Peace ends conflict forever."

Understanding the Process

Thomas and the others began by discussing the first four verses of James and describing some of their own experiences with both positive and negative conflict outcomes. Thomas pointed out that sometimes things get worse before they get better, which was true of Joseph's experience. "But we must learn to take the long view of faith," he said. "Our natural response to conflict is not pure joy!" Everyone laughed in agreement.

Jenny quoted Hebrews 11:1: "Faith is the assurance of things hoped for, the conviction of things not seen." No one disagreed.

"We're going to be looking at a case study soon, but before we do, I want to provide an overview of the model we're using," Thomas explained. He told the group that their approach would view conflict as potentially originating on five different levels, and he asked them to refer to the chart in the notebook he had provided:

1. Intrapersonal
2. Interpersonal
3. Intragroup
4. Intergroup
5. Structural

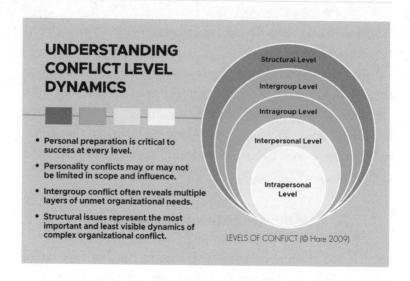

UNDERSTANDING CONFLICT LEVEL DYNAMICS

- Personal preparation is critical to success at every level.
- Personality conflicts may or may not be limited in scope and influence.
- Intergroup conflict often reveals multiple layers of unmet organizational needs.
- Structural issues represent the most important and least visible dynamics of complex organizational conflict.

Structural Level

Intergroup Level

Intragroup Level

Interpersonal Level

Intrapersonal Level

LEVELS OF CONFLICT (© Hare 2009)

"The place to begin is with the smallest circle in the diagram marked *Intrapersonal* dynamics," Thomas said. "This circle represents the part of the conflict residing within us. It includes such things as our emotions, thoughts, spiritual will, and physical health. It also speaks to our frame of mind and our attitudes.

"The next level is the *Interpersonal* sphere. This involves our interactions with one or more people. Restricting this small group to, for example, two to five people allows us to distinguish this level from larger *group dynamics* in conflict captured in the next two levels. These are *Intragroup* and *Intergroup* dynamics. These refer to conflict both within and between groups. The last one pictured is the *Structural* level of conflict.

"We'll also be considering two other aspects of conflict: presenting issues and root causes. Presenting issues are the most visible and easily identifiable symptoms of conflict. Root causes are usually underneath the presenting issues and almost invisible to the casual observer."

Thomas explained that the first sign of trouble usually surfaces at the interpersonal level. Referring to the diagram can help map or sort out the conflicts and discern which steps could be most helpful in identifying root causes, as well as pointing toward possible solutions. Each level of conflict usually requires a different method of intervention. "If the root cause of a conflict is determined to be *intrapersonal*, what might be some of the appropriate intervention strategies to assist this person?" he asked.

Torrey Sanchez, the counseling pastor, replied, "It depends on the problem. Many emotional challenges can be helped with counseling. Certainly, spiritual issues can be addressed there too."

"Great observation!" Thomas replied and then asked, "What about spiritual maturity issues?"

Danika Snyder, the women's ministry director, responded. "Maybe discipling one-on-one, in a triad, or in a small group could help."

"Good. Thanks, Danika." Thomas continued, "What if it is a medical or psychological disorder?"

Barry Gibson, the worship pastor, spoke up this time. "Obviously, getting to the right practitioner or physician." The group nodded in agreement.

After some more discussion, Thomas was ready to move to the next point. "Okay, now let's think about interpersonal conflicts. "If the conflict seems to originate with two—or just a few people—what then?"

"Counseling or mediation might work," Torrey suggested.

"What if the group is larger, let's say involving several families? Or what if there is more than one group at odds with each other, what then?"

Everyone was silent for a moment, thinking. Then Brent Miller, the youth pastor, said, "That gets tricky, I would guess."

Thomas waited to see if anyone else would respond. When no one did, Jenny added, "I remember in a church I was involved in some years ago, the board recommended a congregational meeting for resolving a controversial issue. It was a disaster! It started out okay, but then several people started talking at the same time, then it came to yelling at each other. Others joined in and it got pretty ugly. Within a month, the church split and about a third of the congregation went down the street and started a new church."

Thomas shook his head. "That happens all too often. However, the good news is that there are healthy ways to address group conflict. The key is to structure a process appropriately to the number of people involved. Creating safety and a manageable framework and process is the answer. One good approach is similar to mediation but adapted for the larger group. It is sometimes called problem-solving facilitation. We'll come back to this in more detail later. But there is one more level we need to discuss, which is structural conflicts."

Barry asked, "What do you mean by structural?"

Thomas explained that structural conflict refers to issues that have their origin in organizational policies or procedures or that relate to leadership or social or cultural problems. He added that in churches, theological disagreements also fall into this category. He gave the group a moment to jot down the description in their notes.

"Then that sounds like something only the leadership can resolve," Jenny suggested.

"That's right," Thomas agreed. He continued, "Surprisingly enough, most issues have their root cause in the structural level of conflict, just like most presenting issues show up first in the interpersonal conflict area."

YOUR TURN . . .
EXERCISE

IDENTIFYING THE PRESENTING ISSUE(S)

Consider a complex church conflict either from your own experience or one for which you have detailed information. Using the matrix below, map the characteristics of the conflict by level. What are the presenting issues, and where did they first appear? Keep this case in mind for additional exercises as we move through this model in the pages ahead.

INTRAPERSONAL	INTERPERSONAL	INTRAGROUP	INTERGROUP	STRUCTURAL

UNDERSTANDING THE CONFLICT

Pastor Thomas continued, "Now let's think together about a conflict that took place in our church a number of years ago during a period of rapid growth. Most of you weren't here, but several families began criticizing the decisions of parents who chose schooling options for their children different from their own."

"I remember," Barry said ruefully. "I was here."

Thomas explained that four factions developed—advocates of homeschooling, private Christian school, public school, and charter school. A homeschool group was formed, and Riverdale provided classroom space for them to use periodically. Members of one group began to criticize the parents of another group. Then, some parents whose children were enrolled in a third option began to criticize those choosing other options.

Some Christian school parents insisted that the quality of education among homeschoolers was substandard and provided poor opportunities for socialization. Some of the homeschool parents claimed public school was a worldly and sinful choice for Christian parents to make. Several parents who opted for Christian school pushed back on both the homeschool and public school groups, and they emphasized how Bible classes and Christian standards in their schools made their choice the only one any parent with a Christian conscience could possibly consider. Then parents whose children were enrolled in charter schools reminded everyone of the excellent ratings their schools achieved in specific subjects in which they felt their children were especially gifted. Educational choice even became a topic of discussion in some adult Sunday school classes.

"I remember we lost many families who were offended and who refused to allow our pastoral staff to facilitate reconciliation," Barry said, and added for the benefit of those who had not been there then, "It was a mess."

Thomas continued, "After the fact, we gathered information from those still willing to communicate. I want to revisit this case to see what we might have done differently to provide a better outcome. Let's take a brief coffee break, and when we come back, we'll review that experience and see what we can learn from it."

Chapter 13

Getting Started

Let the wise hear and increase in learning,
and the one who understands obtain guidance.
— Proverbs 1:5

Because I have called and you refused to
listen . . . I also will laugh at your calamity.
— Proverbs 1:24, 26

Gathering Information

Although the issues causing conflict several years before were no longer problematic, Pastor Thomas wanted to head off any similar conflicts and also develop procedures and processes to provide guidance for leaders facing other types of disagreement and potential contention.

After the break, Thomas invited the participants to open their notebooks so they could review transcripts from some of the interviews conducted with parents during the educational choices conflict of several years before. He wanted to discuss how the model might have helped at the time. He reminded them that as is often the case, problems get worse when people talk more than they listen.

He went on to explain that one thing they should have done early on, when they first learned a dispute was brewing, was to invite those involved to meet with the leadership so they would understand the points of view of these parents. Gathering accurate firsthand information could have provided an opportunity for the church leadership to help clarify biblical principles in a healthy and constructive manner instead of allowing gossip and innuendo and criticism to gain the upper hand. "On page one you will see representative excerpts from these interviews," Thomas said.

1. "Public schools are becoming more secular and increasingly immoral in what they are teaching."
2. "We homeschool our kids so we can raise them in the nurture and admonition of the Lord. Isn't this what God commands?"
3. "Christian schools provide biblical content and scriptural codes of conduct to shape and guide our children."
4. "Our kids have all tested as 'gifted,' and we need the focus of a charter school for them to reach their God-given potential."
5. "God gives the responsibility of raising and educating children to their parents, not to the state. Homeschool is the only way to ensure parents fulfill their calling."
6. "I heard a Christian leader, who should know what he is talking about, say Christian schools raise up students who are polished and who know all the right answers but whose hearts are cold and hardened to spiritual things."
7. "Everyone knows homeschooled kids score lower in math and science. How many parents are qualified to teach upper-level technical courses like calculus and physics?"
8. "We homeschool our children, but we don't agree with those who insist it is the *only* Christian choice. Parents have to decide based on a number of factors."
9. "Our kids are in public school as salt and light and to provide a witness. Public school provides opportunities for natural friendships to develop, opening doors of communication and influence. We disciple them at home, but they see their relationships with classmates as ministry opportunities, such as inviting friends to church activities.

How else will these lost children hear about Christ? Besides, not all of us can afford to put our children in Christian schools even if we wanted to!"

YOUR TURN . . .
EXERCISE

DEVELOPING AND CONDUCTING INTERVIEWS

Consider the church conflict selected in the last exercise. What questions might best be asked to get the information needed to comprehensively understand both the presenting and underlying issues (root causes) of this conflict?

INTERVIEW QUESTIONS
1. _____
2. _____
3. _____
4. _____
5. _____

(Use additional paper if needed)

Analyzing the Conflict

Pastor Thomas then asked, "What are your reactions to these statements and questions?"

"I'm sure there is some truth in most of the points made here, but these are generalizations that don't apply in every case," Brent answered.

Thomas continued, "The first presenting issue was an

interpersonal dispute—an argument between two people—that erupted in an adult Sunday school class. But should we therefore assume the root cause of this conflict is isolated to a disagreement between these two parents? Let's map what we see."

INTRAPERSONAL	INTERPERSONAL	INTRAGROUP	INTERGROUP	STRUCTURAL
	Pat and Chris (plus others)			

"If we sat down with these two parties in a counseling or mediation session and they admitted arguing in public is wrong, apologized, said they're sorry, and agreed to disagree in the future, would this church issue be resolved?"

"No," Torrey replied emphatically.

"Why not?" Thomas asked.

"Because these issues run deeper than this one public disagreement," Torrey answered.

"Precisely," Thomas replied. "So let's look at our diagram on the board. We know there are interpersonal conflicts, quite a few, actually. But where else on the conflict level chart do we see issues arising?"

Jenny jumped in. "Intergroup conflict. We have four groups representing four different perspectives."

INTRAPERSONAL	INTERPERSONAL	INTRAGROUP	INTERGROUP	STRUCTURAL
	Pat and Chris (plus others)		Homeschool Public School Christian School Charter School	

"Good," Thomas said as he noted the parties and groups in both the interpersonal and intergroup categories on the board. "Where else do we see disagreements?"

Barry added, "At least one of the homeschool families doesn't agree it is the only right choice. That may mean intragroup conflict also."

"Great insight, Barry!" Thomas replied as he added the intragroup level on the chart.

INTRAPERSONAL	INTERPERSONAL	INTRAGROUP	INTERGROUP	STRUCTURAL
	Pat and Chris (plus others)	Homeschool	Homeschool Public School Christian School Charter School	

"Any other observations?" Thomas asked.

Brent Miller spoke up. "I thought you said most conflicts have their roots in the structural level. What about in this conflict?"

"What about that?" Thomas asked. Only silence. Thomas pressed in. "What are the underlying conditions that allowed this conflict to arise?"

More silence. "It's regretful that most of us don't think deeply into a conflict when it first appears," Thomas said. "There's an opportunity here we missed the first time around. What could we as church leaders have done to have turned this crisis into a teachable moment?"

"Create a platform for these parents to discuss these issues in a healthy way?" Brent suggested.

"Bingo!" Thomas said, pleased. Then he rattled off a round of more questions. "Does the Bible have answers for these types of situations? Is the church a place to help people learn how to make these types of decisions? Could we help our congregation with answering questions like where and how our children should be educated and discipled? Absolutely!" He answered his own questions with conviction and added one more. "So are there any structural issues?"

"It could be viewed as a theological issue," Jenny ventured.

"How so?"

"Well, all these parents seem rightly concerned with their children's spiritual welfare. Some of these statements reflect theological perspective differences. Maybe if the church had provided better learning and communication opportunities, we could have prevented the conflict and encouraged constructive dialogue."

"Thanks, Jenny." Thomas added these new insights on the board.

INTRAPERSONAL	INTERPERSONAL	INTRAGROUP	INTERGROUP	STRUCTURAL
	Pat and Chris (plus others)	Homeschool	Homeschool Public School Christian School Charter School	Teaching and Discipleship training. Communication opportunities for parents.

YOUR TURN . . .
EXERCISE

IDENTIFYING ROOT CAUSES

Drawing on your knowledge of the conflict case you selected above, what indicators do you have that presenting issues might have other underlying root causes? In the matrix below, document these indicators.

INTRAPERSONAL	INTERPERSONAL	INTRAGROUP	INTERGROUP	STRUCTURAL

Designing the Intervention

"Do the rest of you agree with Jenny?" Thomas asked.

"I see her point," Danika said. "These disagreements have structural components because solutions could require leadership intervention. Or, to state it negatively, a part of the reason the problem arose in the first place might be because parents lacked a full understanding of how Scripture can inform important decisions for their family. And if they have a better understanding of the biblical principles involved, they're better equipped to discuss options—in a healthy manner—with other parents whose needs may be different."

"So let's assume these points are correct." Thomas posed additional questions: Once the conflict has surfaced, what steps could be taken to minimize the damage and use the conflict as an opportunity to equip parents? How can the church's culture be impacted in such a way to prevent similar problems in the future? How could the church have created a better environment for parents to wrestle through these matters for themselves and their families?

Then Thomas said, "Let's brainstorm possible strategies that might have improved a leadership response and resulted in a better outcome."

"What if we had created a preaching or teaching series fleshing out what the Bible teaches about parenting and discipling of children?" Torrey asked.

"Thanks, Torrey; let's add that to our list of possibilities," Thomas replied.

"What if we had provided an educational forum to allow for a public discussion of these school choice options for our congregation?" Danika suggested.

Jenny quickly pushed back. "Remember what I said about the congregational meeting that exploded in my previous church. Let's think hard before we go there!"

"Good catch, Jenny, but remember I also said there are ways to structure healthy processes for large group meetings. The key is to create a process to keep things safe for all the participants and still prevent strong emotions from hijacking the meeting. Any ideas?" Thomas asked.

"What about a panel discussion?" Torrey suggested.

"Interesting. Say more."

"Well, with a panel discussion, participants can be carefully selected to ensure they are both knowledgeable and spiritually mature. A skilled facilitator can also keep things on track and head off trouble," Torrey explained. Thomas wrote these suggestions on the board.

INTERVENTION STRATEGIES / RECOMMENDATIONS FOR SOLUTION

1. Preaching/teaching series on biblical parenting

2. Panel discussion on educational choices/rationales

YOUR TURN . . .

EXERCISE

EXPLORING *PREVENTIVE* OPTIONS FOR RESOLUTION

Returning to your own personal case experience, brainstorm some possible *preventive* strategies that might have helped avoid a full-blown conflict. Be sure to include ideas that reach the root cause(s) you have identified.

INTERVENTION STRATEGIES / RECOMMENDATIONS FOR SOLUTION
1.
2.
3.
4.
5.

(Use additional paper if needed)

"These are some good ideas for things we might have done prior to the eruption of the conflict to prevent losing so many people. What about suggestions for strategies to intervene once people are actively engaged in divisive behaviors?" Thomas challenged the group to cite steps that could have been implemented *during* the conflict to help mend fences and reconcile damaged relationships.

Again, only silence as everyone pondered the question. Finally, Danika offered, "Wouldn't the intervention depend on which level of conflict the disagreements come under?"

"Exactly right, Danika, good observation! Looking at our map, let's consider these disagreements one at a time in relation to the level they first appear or are discovered to be. We've already agreed the root causes are structural. So considering what could have helped prior to the conflict might be a good starting place," Thomas replied.

Brent spoke. "If a better understanding of biblical principles is part of what was needed, would our two preventive solution strategies point us in the right direction?"

"Say more, Brent, what are you thinking?" Thomas asked.

"Don't we still need to help these parents learn relevant principles regardless of when and where the conflict arises?"

"Okay, so how would we do this at a point when these parents are already angry with each other?"

"What about the panel discussion idea; could it work here?" Brent asked.

"What do you all think?" Thomas asked, addressing the whole group now.

"A panel discussion might meet the need for education but I am not sure it would be enough to help people manage strong emotions at this stage in the conflict," Torrey replied.

"Pastor, didn't you say there is another process that works for resolving group conflict?" Jenny asked.

"That's right," Danika added, looking at her notes. "Mediation is for resolving interpersonal conflict, and facilitated problem-solving is for helping with groups, correct?"

Thomas agreed. He explained that the more escalated the tensions were in the room, the more structured the process needed to be to help people feel safe and keep communication constructive. Facilitated problem-solving could do both of these through a combination of setting ground rules and guiding the agenda in a managed process so people know what is expected both of themselves and of everyone in the room, including the facilitator.

He continued, "This is probably a good place to remind ourselves that once conflict has emerged on several levels, the intervention design will need to include resources and plans for addressing conflicts at each level." He said that sometimes this could be done simultaneously, but that often the structural level conflict should be addressed first and then whatever conflict remained could be addressed afterward. That is, if enough intervenors are trained, some could work with groups while others are working with individuals. He stressed how important it was to make sure the right people were in the room for each intervention session. "To see how this works, let's turn in our notebooks to our role-play activity for this case and practice some of the skills we will need to learn to be effective."

A word about interviews

In the illustration used here, notes taken during interviews are being used. Interviews can be a useful way to gather information. Here are some helpful considerations and basic guidelines when planning and conducting interviews:

1. A safe environment must be created in order for participants to be willing to provide truthful and complete information. The interviewers should be well-trusted people of integrity and committed to confidentiality.
2. Guidelines should be made clear at the beginning of each session to avoid encouraging gossip and to keep the discussions healthy and constructive.
3. Questions should be open-ended and as neutral as possible. (For sample questions, see Appendix E.)

4. The enrollment process should be designed to be inviting to potential interviewees who have the most accurate information. However, the process should not make people feel unnecessarily excluded. Better too much information than too little.
5. The location for the interviews should be neutral and allow for private access and egress if possible.
6. The interview space and waiting areas should be comfortable, and those facilitating the process should be trusted individuals also.

YOUR TURN . . .
EXERCISE

DEVELOPING STRATEGIES FOR RESOLVING *ACTIVE* CONFLICT

In your case study, think of intervention methods and processes most helpful in addressing the issues identified at each conflict level and record them here.

INTERVENTION STRATEGIES / RECOMMENDATIONS FOR SOLUTION

1. STRUCTURAL

_____

_____

_____

2. INTERGROUP

_____

_____

_____

3. INTRAGROUP

_____

_____

_____

4. INTERPERSONAL

_____

_____

_____

5. INTRAPERSONAL

_____

_____

_____

(Use additional paper if needed)

"Who would like to represent the homeschool position in our role-play?" Thomas asked.

"I will," Barry quickly replied.

"I can represent the Christian school parents," Danika said.

"What about the public school choice—who will take that one?" Pastor Barrington asked.

"I will," Brent replied. "Most of the kids in the youth group attend public schools."

"My kids are in a charter school," Jenny added, "so I'll be happy to represent that group."

"Each of you has four position statements in your notebooks," Thomas explained. "Please read only the description correspond-ing to the position you're representing. I'll facilitate the session, and, Torrey, since you are not assigned a position to defend, would you serve as our neutral observer? You can help us by providing feedback on how we are doing and help us improve our process. Now, let's get started!"

Chapter 14

Guiding the Process Part One: Issues

*What you have heard from me in the presence
of many witnesses entrust to faithful men,
who will be able to teach others also.*
—2 Timothy 2:2

*The facilitator's main task is to help the group increase its
effectiveness by improving its process and structure.*
—Roger Schwarz[36]

"Some additional information might be helpful here."

Thomas reiterated that the larger the group and the more escalated the conflict, the more formal the structure should be. In that day's training exercise, since there were only four participants, one representing each of the four educational choices, one person would serve as the spokesperson for each group. In an actual facilitation, parents from each group would be at the tables.

Thomas said as they worked through the process, he would provide additional information to illustrate the flexibility of the model in accommodating any size group. He added, "I know of one large church conflict where an entire congregation participated from dozens of tables using representatives to speak for each table. They discussed opinions, ideas, recommendations, and so on together, and then the spokesperson at each table represented the group throughout the process."

Thomas directed the participants to the position paper in their notebooks that contained real-life statements from some of the parents representing each of the four positions. He told them they could use those statements to present their position in the role-play. "Please be thinking about how this process could work in other scenarios," he said. "Are we ready to begin?"

Everyone nodded.

Introduce the Process

(This role-play is a fictional account. It's not meant to be a comprehensive representation of parental perspectives or school options but is for illustrative purposes only.)

"Good morning. I will be serving as your facilitator today. I know some strong feelings exist around the topic of schooling choices and that each of you is passionate about raising your children in the nurture and admonition of the Lord. I commend you for that and also for being here today.

"We want to honor Christ both in the way we raise our children and also in the way we resolve issues together. We don't have to agree on everything but we should treat each other in a Christlike manner even if only to agree to disagree. Let's pray and invite the Lord to join us as we move toward these goals."

He prayed that the Holy Spirit would guide the group and that everyone involved would work in the loving manner as instructed in Scripture. After "Amen," Thomas got started.

"Each of you has agreed to allow me to facilitate this discussion today. My goal is to lead in a respectful and constructive manner where everyone feels safe to speak honestly and openly. We've probably all had experiences in group discussions where this did not happen. Group decision-making can be challenging! But as we follow biblical principles, we can better understand each other and the subjects we address. Let's begin by setting some guidelines we can all abide by during our time together," Thomas continued. He said it was important to observe ground rules to help the process run smoothly,[37] and wrote them on the whiteboard.

1. Listen to understand and avoid interrupting.

"If you're anything like me, you sometimes find yourself thinking about what you're going to say next instead of really listening to what the other person is saying. Anyone else do that?"

There were some sheepish smiles around the table.

"Is everyone okay with this guideline?" Pastor Thomas asked. Everyone nodded.

"In front of you are pads and pencils. When you feel tempted to interrupt, please write down your thoughts instead. You'll have an opportunity to return to your concerns and questions once each speaker is finished. The one exception is when you raise your hand to ask a clarifying question. If the person calls on you, you may ask your question. This can help everyone to better understand and also communicates your interest in what is being said if done respectfully. If the person does not call on you, simply write your questions down and ask them later."

Thomas then turned and wrote a second guideline.

2. Remain interested and open to the viewpoints of others. Respectfully test assumptions and inferences.

"I'm always trying to figure other people out, especially those who disagree with me," Thomas continued. "I'm afraid this can lead to my thinking *I really have figured out so-and-so!* The truth is, we can jump to conclusions and make premature judgments. In our discussion today, let's work hard to avoid this mistake and see what we can learn from one another. Often, speakers infer things to be true and assume everyone in the room agrees. It is actually helpful to the group as a whole to respectfully push back or test these assumptions."

3. Share the reasons behind your
statements and questions. Use clear examples.

"It's too easy to judge the motivations of others. We can't constructively respond to what someone says unless we really understand their meaning. Proverbs 18:13 reminds us, 'If one gives an answer before he hears, it is his folly and shame.' By explaining the thinking behind our statements and questions up front, we can help others more fully understand us and help avoid misunderstandings. Another great tool to increase understanding is to provide specific examples."

4. Focus on needs and interests instead of positions.

Thomas wanted to be clear about this point. He said that it was similar to observing the differences between presenting issues and root causes, but that this time they'd be talking about two different levels of focus related to a given problem or statement. He reminded the group that a *position* referred to a specific solution whereas an *interest* described an underlying need.

He used the example of a married couple arguing about how to keep their home safe from intruders. The husband insists on getting a large dog to guard the family residence. The wife instead wants a monitored alarm system for the property. The guard dog and alarm system are specific solutions to consider. They are the *positions* taken by the husband and the wife. However, the underlying need or *interest* is family security.

"Once these needs are recognized and agreed on, a whole host of alternatives may be considered—organizing a neighborhood watch group, moving to a safer neighborhood, and so on. You get the idea." He took a sip of water.

"Next, I want to talk about confidentiality. We have already said we need to create a safe environment to discuss things honestly and without fear of gossip or retaliation. What this requires is for us to protect this process by reassuring each other. Here is a confidentiality agreement form. After we read and discuss the contents and answer any questions, I will ask you to sign and date it where indicated. It is important every participant understands and agrees to these terms of confidentiality for us to be successful. Is everyone comfortable with this requirement? Are there any questions?"

"What if someone refuses to sign the agreement?" Barry asked.

"Today, you're seeing this agreement for the first time. Moving forward, we'll want to teach our leaders and congregation the importance of keeping confidences, and we'll usually have an opportunity to vet our participants to a certain degree beforehand. But in answer to your question—bottom line—if a person is unwilling to commit to confidentiality, they will not be allowed to participate."

"What about talking with our spouses?" Jenny inquired.

"In most cases, even talking with spouses is a violation of the confidentiality agreement. This is not to place undue restraint on married couples but to protect the information and everyone involved. If our spouses are not participants in the process, then they are not able to hear all the information in context. It puts them in an unfair position, and since they have not signed the agreement, it puts them and the process at risk."

Thomas went on, "This is the general rule, but sometimes exceptions might be made on a case-by-case basis, and when that happens, there would need to be a very clear understanding and unanimous agreement about what can and cannot be shared with anyone outside the group. There might be occasions when the spouses could also sign the confidentiality agreement, as long as everything is clear and agreed on by everyone involved. Again, though, this comes under case-by-case situations. Let's move along."

"What's next?" Jenny asked, ready to begin the role-play.

"Good question, and I know I've spent significant time on these guidelines. It has been my experience that anything gained by rushing through these preliminaries is lost through confusion during the facilitation, so thank you for your patience. I think it's easy to feel like we're being sidetracked when we have to spend time in meetings like this one resolving conflict. Let me share with you something I read recently on a blog written by a friend of mine:

> I've heard pastors complain that conflict is interrupting ministry. Programs or projects are slowed down or put on hold because people aren't getting along. As frustrating as this can be, at those times we need to let God remind us that the heart of church isn't programs, but relationships. Jesus didn't say people would know we were his followers by our music, or our sermons, or our programs, but by our love for one another (John 13:35).[38]

"When I read this, I thought about this retreat today. I hope as we continue you'll think of our work here as I have—as time invested and not lost."

Pastor Barrington transitioned to the first PowerPoint slide labeled AGENDA.

---

1. Understand the Issues
    A. What question(s) are we here to answer?
    B. What problem(s) are we here to solve?
2. Establish Common Values
    A. What are our primary values?
    B. What are our secondary values?
3. Explore and Evaluate Current Alternatives
    A. What are our current alternatives?
    B. Are they consistent with biblical values?
4. Define Acceptable Solutions
    A. What can we all agree on?
    B. Are there still unresolved issues?

5. Create an Action Plan

    A. How can we best serve the church?

    B. Who does what and by when?

"Any questions or suggestions regarding the proposed agenda?" Thomas asked. When there were none, he added, "One of the great things about this process is we can make midcourse adjustments along the way by mutual consent if needed. Okay, then, let's get started."

Understand the Issues

"What questions are we here to answer, and what problems are we here to solve? Let's begin by having each group summarize the answers to these two questions from their own vantage points," Thomas directed. "Who would like to go first? And please remember not to interrupt during these opening statements unless you raise your hand to ask for clarification. Otherwise, note your questions and concerns for later in our discussion. Each of your groups will have ample opportunity to do so."

(Sometimes, if tensions are high, either the presentation order can be assigned or randomly selected to prevent further disagreement.)

"If it's okay, I'd like to go first," Barry said.

"If there is no objection, we will start with the homeschool group," Thomas replied. Since no one minded, the pastor signaled for Barry to begin.

"We, as parents, are a very close group," Barry stated. "We meet regularly and collaborate to teach our children. We work mostly as individual family units but sometimes help each other in certain subject areas based on who has the strongest background and education. We believe God has given us the primary responsibility for teaching and discipling our children and, for the most part, we believe it is irresponsible to delegate this duty to anyone or anything else."

Brent interrupted. "Do you really think it's fair to condemn everyone not homeschooling their children?" He was about to continue when Thomas silently pointed to the first ground rule written on the whiteboard: *Listen to understand and avoid interrupting.*

"Oh, sorry," Brent said as he began instead to write his thoughts on the pad in front of him.

Thomas signaled for Barry to continue but asked, "Can you help us understand the first point? What questions are we here to answer, and what problems are we here to solve?"

As Barry answered, Thomas wrote his responses on the large whiteboard. *(Any combination of whiteboards, butcher-paper easels, electronic media tools, etc. that enable legible communication for the group can be used.)*

GROUP	QUESTIONS	PROBLEMS
Homeschool	1. Is homeschooling the only right option for educating and discipling our children? 2. How should we relate to parents who choose a different option?	1. As a church, we haven't provided clear direction for parents to decide biblical alternatives to educate and disciple their children.
Public School		
Christian School		
Charter School		

Guided by the position paper he was using, Barry went on to explain the thinking and conclusions of the parents from the discussion at his table. When he finished, Thomas asked, "Barry, is there anything else you'd like to offer to the group before we move on to our next group's presentation?" Barry looked over his notes and indicated he did not. *(In an actual facilitation, the entire home-school group representatives would be consulted before answering.)*

"Who's next?" Thomas inquired.

Brent spoke up. "I'll go. I'm representing the public school group." Glancing at his notes, he continued, "Christians are supposed to be witnesses for Christ and to provide salt and light to a dark and fallen world. How can we do this if we cloister ourselves away from our lost neighbors? We disciple our children at home and at church and then equip them to be missionaries to their lost friends and teachers. Isn't this a part of what we are supposed to be teaching our children?" Brent was passionate in his support of his group.

He continued, "We're always only one generation from becoming a heathen nation if we fail to evangelize the current one! In addition, we believe we need to help our kids learn to face worldly challenges while they live under our roofs. If we shelter them from the world too much, they won't know how to navigate life when they leave home, go to college, or start their careers. Rather than struggling alone in making difficult decisions about moral choices, we would rather them face some of these questions while they're still living at home and we can help them directly. When they fail and make mistakes, we want to be there to help them mature in their decision-making before they leave home."

Everyone seemed surprised at the intensity coming from their youth pastor and the passion Brent was demonstrating. It was obvious this was more than just a role-play!

As Thomas waited a moment for the others to finish writing down their thoughts, he added Brent's information on the board.

GROUP	QUESTIONS	PROBLEMS
Homeschool	1. Is homeschooling the only right option for educating and discipling our children? 2. How should we relate to parents who choose a different option?	1. As a church, we haven't provided clear direction for parents to decide biblical alternatives to educate and disciple their children.
Public School	1. How can this generation of students and teachers be evangelized if Christian parents remove themselves and their children from public schools? (See also: https://ceai.org.) 2. How can our children learn how to evangelize if we don't allow them to interact with their friends and neighbors at school?	1. As a church, we may not be equipping our congregation to effectively reach their neighbors and to equip their children with the gospel.
Christian School		
Charter School		

"Brent, does this capture your group's main questions and problem statement?" Thomas asked.

"I think so—at least for now," Brent replied.

(The interactions are abbreviated here, but a full discussion should be allowed to take place with enough time provided for the groups to voice their full positions. Rushing through or restricting this process can undermine effectiveness.)

"Jenny, Danika. Who will go next?" Thomas asked. "Do we need a break or shall we continue?"

"Let's continue," Danika said, looking around, and everyone seemed to agree. "May I go next?"

Thomas watched for agreement and nodded for Danika to go ahead.

"I'm representing the Christian school parents," Danika said. "We don't believe our responsibility as parents means we have to do all the teaching and discipling ourselves. Barry, you even admitted a few minutes ago that among homeschool parents you sometimes have the parent who has specific skills or education in certain subject areas to teach all the homeschool children, not just your own."

Barry started to react but remembered the ground rules and began writing instead as Danika continued.

"What about the church? Don't we allow our youth leaders and Sunday school teachers to have a part in discipling our kids? We believe while our children are at home, we have a limited opportunity to make sure they get grounded educationally and spiritually so they are prepared to be salt and light in the world as adults," she said, looking at Brent, who was writing and didn't look up. "A Christian school is the best way to control the learning environment while our children are impressionable and vulnerable. It supplements and reinforces what they're learning at home and church while preventing the worst influences from stealing their hearts away from their parents and from Christ."

GROUP	QUESTIONS	PROBLEMS
Homeschool	1. Is homeschooling the only right option for educating and discipling our children? 2. How should we relate to parents who choose a different option?	1. As a church, we haven't provided clear direction for parents to decide biblical alternatives to educate and disciple their children.
Public School	1. How can this generation of students and teachers be evangelized if Christian parents remove themselves and their children from public schools? 2. How can our children learn how to evangelize if we don't allow them to interact with their friends and neighbors at school?	1. As a church, we may not be equipping our congregation to effectively reach their neighbors and community children with the gospel.
Christian School	1. Are parents biblically responsible for directly providing all instruction to their children? 2. If not, what alternative resources are legitimate options?	1. See above statements
Charter School		

"Anything else, Danika?"

"No, if we can find answers to those questions, I believe it will help all of us find better solutions," she concluded.

Thomas said, "Great. Okay, Jenny, we need to hear from you and the charter school parents now."

Jenny said, "Thank you for helping us understand why each of you as parents have made the decisions you have for educating your children. I hope I can do the same for all of you regarding our group's choices. We share the same concerns, believing God has entrusted our children to us as gifts from Him to love and steward with His guidance. Our world is becoming more technical and specialized as far as what kind of educational needs our children have. As Christian parents, we are of course most concerned for their spiritual welfare." She glanced at her notes and went on.

"Those of us who choose charter schools take the discipling responsibility very seriously but believe between what our children learn at home and church, we can also take advantage of educational resources available in the community. Most public schools are restricted to a standardized educational regimen. Charter schools historically allow parents more control in selection of curriculum, budget allocation, administration, and more. By focusing on certain subjects like math and science, these schools also provide higher quality education in these specialties. So, in our community at least, as parents we can select the best schools to match our children's gifts and interests."

GROUP	QUESTIONS	PROBLEMS
Homeschool	1. Is homeschooling the only right option for educating and discipling our children? 2. How should we relate to parents who choose a different option?	1. As a church, we haven't provided clear direction for parents to decide biblical alternatives to educate and disciple their children.
Public School	1. How can this generation of students and teachers be evangelized if Christian parents remove themselves and their children from public schools? 2. How can our children learn how to evangelize if we don't allow them to interact with their friends and neighbors at school?	1. As a church, we may not be equipping our congregation to effectively reach their neighbors and community children with the gospel.
Christian School	1. Are parents biblically responsible for directly providing all instruction to their children? 2. If not, what alternative resources are legitimate options?	1. See above statements
Charter School	1. Where can our children receive the highest quality education, especially in technical subjects? 2. Where can parents exercise the greatest influence on curriculum, budget, administration, and so on?	1. See above statements

"Great summary. Is there anything else you would like to add, Jenny?" Thomas asked.

"No, I think my main points are now on the board, thanks," Jenny replied.

Thomas continued. "Okay, I know you each are thinking of additional things you wish to say. I can tell by how busy you have been writing on your note pads! As we move through the agenda, we'll have opportunity to explore these questions and problem statements together and to work on gaining a better understanding of each other while developing ideas to strengthen our church ministries in addressing these very important questions and issues for the future." Thomas and his staff continued to flesh out the positions and interests for each group. They were now ready to talk about values.

YOUR TURN . . .
EXERCISE

SUMMARIZE POSITIONS AND ISSUES

In your own conflict case, list the primary questions to answer and problems to solve from each group's perspective. Sometimes they will overlap or be the same. These issues can be sorted out as you move through the process.

GROUP	QUESTIONS	PROBLEMS
Group One	1. 2. 3.	1. 2. 3.
Group Two	1. 2. 3.	1. 2. 3.
Group Three	1. 2. 3.	1. 2. 3.
Group Four	1. 2. 3.	1. 2. 3.

(Use additional paper if needed)

Chapter 15

Guiding the Process
Part Two: Values

*It is honorable for a man to stop
striving, since any fool can start a quarrel.*
—Proverbs 20:3 NKJV

*Compassion means adopting a stance toward others
and yourself in which you temporarily suspend judgment.*[39]
—Roger Schwarz

One of the great benefits of Christians working together to solve problems is we share so many values, especially on moral and ethical issues. Since the Bible is our standard of faith and practice, it provides common ground and creates a foundation on which to build. For this stage in the process, we will consider *primary* and *secondary* values. The difference between these two sets of principles has to do with those values held as absolute and those held as discretionary. Within the Christian community, this distinction may differ slightly between denominational groups or other traditions, so it is important to define these categories within the distinctives of the particular groups involved.

One scriptural example can be found in these two verses: Hebrews 10:24–25 reads, "Let us consider how to stir up one another to love and good works, not neglecting to meet together, as is the habit of some, but encouraging one another, and all the more as you see the Day drawing near." Compare this verse to Romans

14:5, which reads, "One person esteems one day as better than another, while another esteems all days alike. Each one should be fully convinced in his own mind."

Hebrews 10:25 is generally accepted as a strong directive by God to participate regularly in some form of corporate gathering. We could say this is a *primary* value because it elevates meeting regularly to a biblical expectation many would see as absolute. On the other hand, Romans 14:5 indicates that God extends latitude in how Christians view the importance of any particular day. One Christian might view Sunday as a special or even a sacred day unlike any other day of the week. A second Christian might consider every day of the week of equal importance, including Sunday. This Scripture allows for Christians to agree to disagree on this point without either party sinning.

In much the same way, we might say preaching and teaching the Bible is of *primary* importance. However, whether it is preached on Saturday or Sunday, or in an auditorium or a living room, or in a live service or over the airwaves is of *secondary* importance. Unfortunately, Christians often engage in conflict over secondary issues when God allows divergence of opinion on a particular issue. Helping parties recognize and agree on these distinctions can frequently move them toward resolution and reconciliation through agreeing to disagree when no sin is involved.

Establish Common Values

After explaining these distinctions, Pastor Thomas asked, "How do primary and secondary values enter into how we educate and disciple our children?" When he got no response, he rephrased: "Let me ask it a different way: what values can we agree are primary to our discussion today?"

Jenny replied, "Parents have a great responsibility before God to raise their children in the nurture and admonition of the Lord."

"Say more about that; any examples?" Thomas asked as he pointed to the third ground rule: *Share the reasons behind your statements and questions. Use clear examples.*

"All four groups clearly believe discipling and educating our children is a God-given responsibility. These activities are a part of obeying God's directive," Jenny said.

"Any disagreement?" Thomas asked and wrote on the board.

PRIMARY VALUES	SECONDARY VALUES
1. Parental responsibility to raise children in nurture and admonition of the Lord. This includes the discipling and educating of our children.	

With no objections, Thomas continued. "Are there any other primary values at stake here?"

Brent added, "This responsibility includes equipping our children to be evangelists while at the same time protecting them appropriately from evil."

Again Thomas asked, "Any disagreement?" With none voiced, he added these notes to the board.

PRIMARY VALUES	SECONDARY VALUES
1. Parental responsibility to raise children in nurture and admonition of the Lord. This includes the discipling and educating of our children.	
2. Equipping children to evangelize.	
3. Appropriate protection of our children from evil.	

The staff members continued adding examples to the list of the biblical principles they considered primary to all parents regarding their children. .

Thomas then said, "Great job! You've identified critical primary issues we can all agree on. Next, do you see any related values that could be seen as secondary in answering the questions and resolving the problems we're considering today?"

Brent suggested, "Isn't it possible to make different school choices and still be faithful to the primary values on the board?"

"Go on," Thomas encouraged.

Brent continued, "For example, not all parents or family circumstances are the same. Not all children are the same. Not all schools are the same. It seems to me the principles are primary, but the means and methods could be considered secondary."

"Interesting. Your point raises several questions that merit discussion within your groups," Thomas replied. "If we were in an actual facilitation with several parents in each group, this would be a good place to take whatever time is needed to encourage our groups to discuss this and see if they could come to any conclusions about Brent's point. Since we don't have those parents here today, read through the comments listed in your position paper to see if anyone supports viewing primary and secondary values this way."

Brent read from his notes. "One parent stated, 'We live outside of town in an independent school system. Although we've heard urban school districts are mandated to teach a standardized curriculum on sexual orientation and gender issues, our schools have continued teaching traditional family values, and most of our teachers and administrators are openly Christian in their words and actions.'"

"How does this connect to our current question?" Thomas asked.

Barry raised his hand and Thomas motioned for him to respond. "It was the gender issue mandate that motivated us to pull our kids out of the public schools," Barry replied. "If we had public school options supportive of our family values, some of our homeschoolers would probably still be in the public schools."

"Thank you, Barry," Thomas replied as he wrote on the board.

PRIMARY VALUES	SECONDARY VALUES
1. Parental responsibility to raise children in nurture and admonition of the Lord. This includes the discipling and educating of our children.	1. Methods and means of education are secondary and subject to options available in different locales.
2. Equipping children to evangelize.	
3. Appropriately protecting our children from evil.	

Thomas asked Barry if what he had written reflected his point about secondary values.

"It does for me. There are some in our group who insist

homeschooling is the only way to make sure parents can maintain adequate control of the curriculum and values being taught, but as a group we can see how parents could make a different choice if circumstances were favorable enough," Barry replied.

Thomas went to the next primary value on the chart. "What about the issue of evangelism?"

Danika responded, "For those of us in Christian schools, we believe it is important for our children to interact with unsaved neighbors and friends. Some of the Christian schools in our area provide service projects to create opportunities for evangelism. And, even for those that don't, most evangelical churches in town have evangelistic outreaches and short-term mission trips for this purpose." Thomas recorded this information as he asked for additional input.

PRIMARY VALUES	SECONDARY VALUES
1. Parental responsibility to raise children in nurture and admonition of the Lord. This includes the discipling and educating of our children.	1. Methods and means of education are secondary and subject to options available in different locales.
2. Equipping children to evangelize.	2. Platforms and channels to equip youth for evangelism are secondary.
3. Appropriately protecting our children from evil.	

Jenny spoke. "Speaking for the charter school parents, we just discussed this issue of protecting our kids from the evil influences in the world. This can be a tough one! We want to do all we can to protect them, but we also know sooner or later we're not going to be around to help. And besides, Christ calls us to engage our culture with the gospel. Some of our charter schools are overtly

Christian. Others are part of the public school system and clearly are secular in their orientation."

Jenny glanced at her notes, then added, "There should be a balance between overprotecting and putting our kids at risk. But after hearing from each of the other groups, parents must prayerfully find a balance in our own circumstances. Discipling our kids means making decisions about all the primary and secondary values areas discussed today. It seems like we're concluding that these decisions belong to the parents. Does everyone agree?"

No one disagreed that in the end parents were responsible for making decisions about their own family.

"Thank you, Jenny!" Thomas said and wrote down the following comments.

PRIMARY VALUES	SECONDARY VALUES
1. Parental responsibility to raise children in nurture and admonition of the Lord. This includes the discipling and educating of our children.	1. Methods and means of education are secondary and subject to options available in different locales.
2. Equipping children to evangelize.	2. Platforms and channels to equip youth for evangelism are secondary.
3. Appropriately protecting our children from evil.	3. Dangers vary from community to community and require different precautions. Balancing of factors to meet primary values may differ for each family, indicating that the methods are secondary.

"How are we doing?" Thomas asked.

After a momentary pause, Barry raised his hand, and Thomas nodded for him to speak. Barry explained that they still had families in the homeschool group who very strongly believed homeschooling is the best option for every family.

"But," Barry added, "I think generally there would be a willingness to agree to disagree on these secondary issues while agreeing
on the primary ones."

Thomas waved his hand to the whole group. "What about the
rest of you?"

Brent spoke up next. "I've learned some things today. As youth
pastor, I see a very diverse group of parents making decisions for
their kids. Most are members of our church, and others are out-
siders who only drop off their children for activities. But I agree
with Jenny. Most of the parents I know care deeply about their
children's education and their spiritual welfare. I think the best
thing we can do is listen to one another and be supportive of the
educational choices other parents make even if we don't know all
the reasons for their choices."

"Danika, what about the Christian school parents—where do
you think they land on these issues?" Thomas asked.

"As I read the comments here from our parents and talk with
those who have their children in Christian school, I know we have
some who are dogmatic about their beliefs on this question. However, if they could have been a part of the discussion today, I believe most would respect the choices of parents making different
decisions than they do on these issues. We'll always have some
people who take extreme positions, but I believe as a church, we
can help equip parents to evaluate their options and decide in their
own circumstances—while also respecting the choices of others."

"A perfect transition to our next agenda point!" Thomas said.
"Much of the heavy lifting is done, and I believe we have turned a
corner. We can now move to finding good solutions."

YOUR TURN . . .
EXERCISE

IDENTIFYING PRIMARY AND SECONDARY ISSUES

Thinking of your conflict case, identify biblical issues and separate them into primary and secondary value categories based on the criteria defined above.

PRIMARY VALUES	SECONDARY VALUES
1.	1.
2.	2.
3.	3.
4.	4.

(Use additional paper if needed)

Chapter 16

Guiding the Process Part Three: Finding Solutions

He guards the paths of justice, and preserves the way of His saints.
—Proverbs 2:8 NKJV

A man's heart plans his way, but the LORD directs his steps.
—Proverbs 16:9 NKJV

"You're all doing great!" Thomas said. "It is important to remember this model does not represent a single event but represents a process. The time line can vary greatly, and it is more important to do it well than do it fast."

He went on to explain the concept of "process satisfaction," which is critical to effectiveness and reaching good outcomes. In the busyness of a breakneck culture, people want instant results. But in the world of conflict resolution, the key is allowing enough time for participants to carefully work through all the important issues. The larger the group, the longer this usually takes. Any issues left unresolved can unravel any benefits and undermine a healthy outcome.

One person said, "That almost seems daunting to expect anything to be resolved."

Thomas responded, "A lot of it is attitude. If we look at conflict resolution and problem-solving as a distraction and not worth much in terms of actual ministry, you're right! But if we look at the process as a ministry, our attitude changes."

He explained the benefits of viewing conflict resolution as an opportunity for a church to get back on track but also as an opportunity for transformational change for the people participating in the process and even for the entire congregation. "I think you will agree when you see how a process like this can bring new insights and equip us not just for one issue but for future issues as well. Let's look at what we know so far."

The participants quickly reviewed their progress and after a few clarifying questions agreed to move to the next topic.

Explore and Evaluate Current Options

"Our next step is to look at and evaluate available options—in this case, for educating and discipling our children. For our current conflict, most of this has already been done. So let's look at our four alternatives again and evaluate them in light of Scripture and what we have learned. The four options we have been discussing are homeschool, public school, Christian school, and charter school. Are there any others we need to add?" Thomas asked.

Jenny replied, "There are options like military or boarding schools and in some districts alternative schools. But I think the principles and methods in our current four choices would work for these other options."

The other participants indicated they agreed with Jenny.

"Okay, here is our matrix for further evaluation," Thomas continued, and outlined it on the board.

CRITERIA	HOMESCHOOL	PUBLIC SCHOOL	CHRISTIAN SCHOOL	CHARTER SCHOOL
Educating and discipling	Strengths: Challenges:	Strengths: Challenges:	Strengths: Challenges:	Strengths: Challenges:
Equipping for evangelism	Strengths: Challenges:	Strengths: Challenges:	Strengths: Challenges:	Strengths: Challenges:
Protecting from evil	Strengths: Challenges:	Strengths: Challenges:	Strengths: Challenges:	Strengths: Challenges:

"Here are the options we're discussing. Let's summarize our points so far and add any further thinking on these issues," the pastor suggested.

"Maybe there's some overlap," Torrey observed. "It would seem evangelism is a part of discipleship."

"I agree," Brent replied. "But it was distinctly mentioned in connection with differing school choices, so I think we should treat them as two things."

When no one objected, Thomas went on, "Let's record as concisely as possible our reflections in each category." He filled in the matrix as they collectively offered information.

CRITERIA	HOMESCHOOL	PUBLIC SCHOOL	CHARTER SCHOOL	CHRISTIAN SCHOOL
Educating and discipling	Strengths: One-on-one student interaction; control of curriculum; flexible scheduling Challenges: Quality of instruction; socialization	Strengths: Socialization; economy Challenges: Mandated curriculum; quality of instruction	Strengths: Parental involvement; quality instruction Challenges: Negative influences	Strengths: Consistent training and instruction Challenges: Cost; potential isolation from other perspectives
Equipping for evangelism	Strengths: Parental training and modeling Challenges: Potential isolation; some parents might neglect this	Strengths: Daily interaction with the lost Challenges: Potential restrictions and retaliation	Strengths: Daily interaction with the lost (in some cases) Challenges: Potential restrictions and retaliation	Strengths: Potential training Challenges: Potential isolation
Protecting from evil	Strengths: Control of environment Challenges: Potential isolation	Strengths: Opportunities for teaching discernment Challenges: Negative influences; indoctrination	Strengths Socialization; economy Challenges: Negative influences (in some cases)	Strengths: Christian students and teachers Challenges: Potential isolation , from other perspectives

"This is certainly not exhaustive, but what are your reactions to seeing this information put together in this way?" Thomas asked.

"It's instructive," Torrey replied. "Seeing it organized this way offers a more balanced opportunity for evaluation."

"What are your conclusions, then?" Thomas asked.

Brent and Barry started to speak at the same time, and Barry motioned for Brent to go ahead.

"I think this reinforces our earlier perspectives—by offering balance to the discussion and furthering grace and understanding toward those making different choices."

"But how would this resolve the conflict that had been in our church?" Jenny asked.

"I'm glad you asked," Thomas responded with a smile.

YOUR TURN . . .
EXERCISE

EXPLORING AND IDENTIFYING EVALUATION CRITERIA

Reflecting on your conflict case, explore and identify best alternatives and biblical criteria to evaluate your options based on the principles defined in this chapter.

CRITERIA	OPTION 1	OPTION 2	OPTION 3	OPTION 4
1.	Strengths: Challenges:	Strengths: Challenges:	Strengths: Challenges:	Strengths: Challenges:
2.	Strengths: Challenges:	Strengths: Challenges:	Strengths: Challenges:	Strengths: Challenges:
3.	Strengths: Challenges:	Strengths: Challenges::	Strengths: Challenges:	Strengths: Challenges:

(Use additional paper if needed)

Define Acceptable Solutions

"What can we all agree on? And are there still unresolved issues?" Thomas inquired.

"We all agree that any of these four options can be legitimate and biblical if chosen for the right reasons and in the right circumstances," Danika offered.

"How many agree with this?" Thomas asked.

Jenny was slow to raise her hand. "Am I seeing hesitation, Jenny?" Thomas asked.

"In general, *I* agree, but I don't believe all our parents would agree," Jenny explained. "If they had all been present today and had an opportunity to see and hear what we've experienced, perhaps most would. But they're not here. And what about those whose relationships have already been damaged?"

"These are great questions, and I'm glad you asked them, Jenny!" Thomas replied. "This is just a role-play. Our goal today is to learn the process and to revisit in our imagination what might have been done in the past that would have resulted in a better outcome for our church. So think with me about next steps if we were actually gathering as a church staff with our parents at the time of this conflict. Working together, what should we do next?"

He reminded the group that their agenda called for them to identify areas of agreement and also to recognize areas of unresolved conflict. Most important, he told them, they needed to regard the directive called Define Acceptable Solutions. He said they would next brainstorm how to translate what had been achieved in the facilitation into practical solutions and action points—the next steps in the process. Thomas referred to the graphic he pulled up on the screen.

"Remember the Levels of Conflict diagram? This is a tool to help us sort out and choose interventions at the appropriate levels of conflict remaining in our congregation."

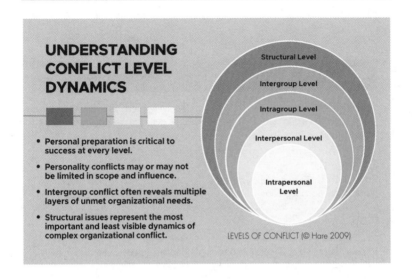

UNDERSTANDING CONFLICT LEVEL DYNAMICS

- Personal preparation is critical to success at every level.
- Personality conflicts may or may not be limited in scope and influence.
- Intergroup conflict often reveals multiple layers of unmet organizational needs.
- Structural issues represent the most important and least visible dynamics of complex organizational conflict.

Structural Level
Intergroup Level
Intragroup Level
Interpersonal Level
Intrapersonal Level

LEVELS OF CONFLICT (© Hare 2009)

"Perhaps you remember that the outer circle labeled Structural is where most root causes can be found. You may also remember if solutions are found at this level, conflict is potentially greatly reduced in other levels. This level is also primarily the sphere requiring leadership involvement to define and implement solutions."

He waited a bit to ensure everyone was with him before he went on. "Assuming we selected parents who were spiritually mature and influential in the best sense—truly representative of the other parents in their respective school choice groups—for our facilitated problem-solving session, what might be a next step to extend their newfound knowledge to the rest of the congregation? In addition, what other conflicts can we identify that exist (or would have existed at that time) on the other levels on the diagram?"

Thomas asked these questions and then recorded the group's suggestions.

LEVEL OF CONFLICT	INTERVENTION
STRUCTURAL Education is needed congregation-wide	Teaching, preaching, group meetings, public panel discussion
INTERGROUP Homeschool group has open conflict with public school group	Facilitated problem-solving session
INTRAGROUP Homeschool group is divided between homeschool only and those open to other options	Multiparty mediation or facilitated problem-solving session (depending on number of affected members)
INTERPERSONAL Multiple—to be identified	Mediation and/or counseling/coaching
INTRAPERSONAL Attitudinal/spiritual/psychological—to be identified	Counseling, coaching, therapy

"Your recommendations are right on track!" Thomas continued, pleased with their progress. "One of the advantages of this model is that it can be modified and adjusted to meet changing conditions. As hidden or emerging issues and needs are discovered, midcourse adjustments can be made to address changing dynamics as they appear. But we have to start somewhere. So let's move to the action plan!"

ANALYZING MULTILEVEL CONFLICT

In your own conflict case, identify the level where each conflict is located and recommend specific intervention strategies and methods.

LEVEL OF CONFLICT	INTERVENTION
STRUCTURAL	
INTERGROUP	
INTRAGROUP	
INTERPERSONAL	
INTRAPERSONAL	

(Use additional paper if needed)

Create an Action Plan

"Okay, now it's time to put together an action plan." He drew their attention to the fifth item in the agenda. "How can we best serve the church? and Who does what and by when?" Thomas asked.

Thomas encouraged his staff to volunteer for the tasks they

felt best qualified and gifted for. Date ranges were chosen with flexibility because of the need to coordinate participant calendars. Agreement was made to monitor progress in weekly staff meetings and finalize accordingly.

STAFF MEMBER	ASSIGNMENT	DUE DATE
Thomas (senior pastor)	Oversee the development of strategy to inform and equip parents regarding educational and discipling responsibilities and options. Work with staff to select panel discussion participants to best represent each group. Facilitate panel discussion.	March 2–May 20 or until completed
Jenny (Christian ed director)	Work with staff, lay leaders, and congregation to schedule approved meetings and events.	March 2–May 20 or until completed
Danika (women's ministry director)	Facilitate problem-solving sessions within and between groups (except for homeschool intragroup session since Barry is a trusted parent in this group).	As scheduled April 2–May 20 or until completed
Brent (youth pastor)	Facilitate informational meetings and any mediation or problem-solving sessions with youth (requires parent input and approval slips).	April 2–May 20 or until completed
Barry (worship pastor)	Facilitate homeschool intragroup session (of which he is a part).	As soon as it can be scheduled

Torrey (counseling pastor)	Conduct counseling, coaching, and mediation sessions as needed. Research mediation curriculums.	April 2–May 20 or until completed

YOUR TURN . . .
EXERCISE

CREATING AN ACTION PLAN

Reflecting on your conflict case, identify best key leaders (or if it is a case from the past, those who would have been most effective) to organize and facilitate problem-solving sessions, mediations, counseling sessions, referrals, and so on. Set dates or date ranges and accountability checkpoints.

STAFF MEMBER	ASSIGNMENT	DUE DATE
1.		
2.		
3.		
4.		
5.		

6.		

(Use additional paper if needed)

Thomas looked over the schedule on the board and then turned to his staff. "What do you think?"

"This has been very helpful to me," Barry replied. "Our home-school parents are some of the most passionate people I've ever met regarding their children. I think a process like this could greatly help them understand and appreciate the educational decisions of other church families."

Danika agreed. "Our Christian school parents are also very invested in choosing Christian school for their kids, but this would have been helpful."

Jenny said, "This has been good for us, but how can we as church leaders integrate this process into the culture of our church? We still have present conflicts, and more are bound to arise in the future."

"Thanks, Jenny, that is exactly the right question to ask and after we break for lunch, we'll get started on finding the answer!" Thomas stated confidently.

Chapter 17

Building the Team Part One: People and Resources

*By the grace given to me I say to everyone among you not
to think of himself more highly than he ought to think,
but to think with sober judgment, each according
to the measure of faith that God has assigned.*
—Romans 12:3

*Having gifts that differ according to the grace given to us,
let us use them . . . in proportion to our faith.*
—Romans 12:6

Identify Potential Peacemakers

Why build a team for a peacemaking ministry? As we have demonstrated throughout this book, conflict is a normal part of life—even church life! And, as difficult as conflict can be, conflict also creates opportunities. Frequently, churches have conflict-avoidant cultures, making conflict and conflict resolution a taboo subject. Healthy church leaders and healthy cultures welcome and engage conflict as a necessary part of kingdom ministry.

Leading cultural change is a challenging but necessary objective when the prevalent culture is unhealthy and conflict avoidant. The dynamics of conflict and the constructive strategies illustrated in this book can open doors for creative and needed change; we saw this demonstrated in the early church in Acts 6:1–7. Individuals, no matter how charismatic or gifted, seldom change organizational culture single-handedly.[40] It takes a team, and building a team is all about getting the right people in the right places.

We all have gifts from God, fitting us for certain tasks and responsibilities. While not everyone interested in conflict resolution is well-suited for all aspects of this ministry, opportunities other than working directly with the disputing parties are available. There is room for any number of gifts on the team, and some of those roles don't require mediating between parties; some tasks are more relational and some are more administrative. Although no single gift is defined in Scripture as a "peacemaking gift," some gifts are more essential for helping people navigate conflict than others (see chapter 11).

Existing relationships sometimes factor into the selection process also. The selection of the seven men in Acts 6 reflected spiritual, relational, and cultural qualifications and relationships.

Let's look again at the roles assigned by Pastor Thomas from the last chapter and consider possible rationales in selecting each member's position on the team:

STAFF MEMBER	ASSIGNMENT	RATIONALE
Thomas (senior pastor)	Oversee the development of strategy to inform and equip parents regarding educational and discipling responsibilities and options. Work with staff to select panel discussion participants to best represent each group. Facilitate panel discussion.	Thomas's primary gift is pastor/teacher and his second is administration. As senior pastor, Thomas is in the best position to oversee the project since it involves a churchwide conflict. He also has proven leadership and facilitation skills, and has good working relationships with his staff.

Jenny (Christian ed director)	Work with staff, lay leaders, and congregation to schedule approved meetings and events.	Jenny's top two gifts are tied with administration and serving. As the Christian ed director, she is respected and trusted, and she has proven that she can work cross-functionally with the whole congregation.
Danika (women's ministry director)	Facilitate problem-solving sessions within and between groups (except for homeschool intragroup session since Barry is a trusted parent in this group).	Danika is gifted in organizing and facilitating small-group women's ministries in the church. She has shown patience and grace, along with strong interpersonal skills.
Brent (youth pastor)	Facilitate informational meetings and any mediation or problem-solving sessions with youth (requires parents' input and approval slips).	The youth ministry has encountered turbulent conflict involving both youth and parents. Brent has successfully kept the lines of communication open and resolved most issues through informal negotiation and mediation.
Barry (worship pastor)	Facilitate homeschool intragroup session (of which he is a part).	Barry has served as a leader among parents in the homeschool group and has built strong relationships with both sides in the intragroup conflict.
Torrey (counseling pastor)	Conduct counseling, coaching, and mediation sessions as needed. Research mediation curriculms.	Torrey's primary gift is mercy. His ability to empathize seems balanced with his leadership gifts to provide direct but gentle guidance to people in crisis. His counseling education included training in family mediation.

Set the Course

"Okay, I trust everyone enjoyed the great food that was provided. Who remembers where we left off?" Thomas asked.

Torrey spoke up. "We were about to tackle Jenny's question—how we can use what we've learned to equip the whole congregation for future challenges."

"Yes," Thomas confirmed. "We've got a good game plan to educate our church on school choice, which will hopefully prevent further conflict. Using what we've learned, we should be able to strengthen our ministry to parents and students going forward."

He urged the staff members to think beyond the current issue of discussion and instead work on how they could equip the church to better handle other types of misunderstandings and disagreements in the future. In their various roles, they would be responsible to lead and mentor the process, but he wanted them to explore how they could pass the knowledge and these skills they were learning beyond themselves and to others in the congregation. "Any ideas on how we might do that?" he asked.

Torrey was the first to speak. "I'm thinking there must be a good way to measure interest in this type of ministry—perhaps a survey of some sort?"

"Or could we offer some training to see who responds?" Jenny suggested.

"Both are good ideas. Are there any others?" Thomas wanted to get as many ideas as possible.

"Maybe we could look for people whose career involves conflict resolution or those who have already received training in these types of skills," Barry suggested.

"These are all great ideas," Thomas replied. "How do we decide which ones to pursue?"

Thomas and his staff discussed the pros and cons and decided to offer a thirteen-week curriculum in biblical conflict resolution as one of the electives to be scheduled during the weekly Bible study hour at the church. This would allow staff to provide an overview of the topic while also getting to observe the gifting and potential of those who participated. They could then develop a more in-depth, continuing education training curriculum that would be required for those who would serve in actual mediation roles on the team.[41] A next logical step would be to conduct a spiritual gift assessment to get an idea of which people could use their gifts to serve in different roles on the conflict resolution team.

For Independent and Smaller Churches

Independent churches may or may not have intervention resources available from an association or fellowship network. In these cases, church conflict or church health organizations can offer assistance. Smaller churches will normally need only one or two people to serve in these roles. Sometimes an invitation to do something this unique catches the attention of individuals or couples who have not been involved in church ministry but who have the right background, experience, and/or gifts. Mediation and facilitation training doesn't have to be structured in a class format but can be done through self-study, one-on-one, or in small groups. If no suitable individuals are found within the congregation, volunteers can sometimes be identified outside the church (either from other churches or from community mediation centers or colleges). Church conflict consulting firms can also offer training, coaching, and intervention services.

Training and Practice

After some discussion, Thomas and his staff agreed that assessing spiritual gifts would be a helpful step in building a team. And they decided the first class could serve as a pilot group to evaluate the curriculum and watch for potential team members. Since Thomas and Torrey have the most experience in resolving conflicts, they will colead the first class and retake a spiritual gift assessment inventory that will later be used for future candidates. They also decided, assuming the pilot was successful, to call this process the Healthy Community Team training program and drafted the following charter document:

Healthy Community Team[42]

Name
The name of this team will be the Healthy Community Team (HCT).

Member commitment
Members commit to serve for a term of twelve months. Terms may be shortened or extended in consultation with church leadership.

Role of the Healthy Community Team
The Healthy Community Team is a conflict resolution ministry team responsible to help identify, intervene, and assist in the healthy resolution of interpersonal and systemic church conflicts. Except as specifically authorized by the church's governing board, the Healthy Community Team will only advise, coach, mediate, and facilitate church disputes; they will have no authority to legislate or make policy. The Healthy Community Team will also monitor implementation of recommendations once action steps have been authorized, providing accountability.

Main Communication Channels
The Healthy Community Team will work closely with:
• Our senior pastor
• Our governing board
• Leader(s) assigned to shepherd this ministry.

Membership Requirements
1. Successfully complete the thirteen-week conflict resolution training prior to appointment. Agree to continuing education while serving.
2. Complete a spiritual gift assessment survey prior to appointment.
3. Receive approval from authorized HCT ministry leadership.[43]
4. Sign and date Team Agreement and Confidentiality forms.

Team Responsibilities
1. Pray regularly for the success of the reconciliation ministry of the HCT.

2. Work individually and as a team to help identify and intervene in unhealthy interpersonal and systemic church conflicts.
3. Recognize and respond to unhealthy disagreements and disputes within the congregation by invitation or by appointment.
4. Utilize approved processes and procedures as trained and directed.
5. Be available to assist in educating the congregation and participating in church training opportunities.
6. Make specific recommendations (without violating confidences) for improving training and developing best practices.
7. Identify areas where training and coaching are needed and facilitate training events and coaching.
8. Keep the leadership informed of the team's work.

Adoption of Charter
This charter was approved by the Elder Board on _____ (date).

"Again, great work!" Thomas said. "Let's talk now about the curriculum for this class. What are your ideas?"

Danika knew of a church that used an eight-session video course[44] and offered to look into it before the next meeting.

"Great! Any other resources anyone else is aware of?" Thomas asked.

Torrey said, "I have some books from my counseling training that might help. I can review what I find and bring those to our next meeting too."

During that week, Danika was able to borrow the videos from her colleague in a neighboring church and watch the whole series, and Torrey found helpful resources in his personal library.

As they concluded the final segment of that day's retreat, Pastor Barrington and his staff committed to research available Christian resources to determine how to structure their course content. They also decided to initiate the implementation of these principles to stimulate healthy dialogue among all the interested parents in the church. In the next chapter, we will join them again a couple of weeks later as they meet to review their school choice plans and develop a framework to create a Healthy Community Team for their church.

Chapter 18

Building the Team Part Two: Planning the Course

I therefore, a prisoner for the Lord, urge you to walk in a manner worthy of the calling to which you have been called, with all humility and gentleness, with patience, bearing with one another in love, eager to maintain the unity of the Spirit in the bond of peace.
—Ephesians 4:1–3

Speaking the truth in love, we are to grow up in every way into him who is the head, into Christ, from whom the whole body, joined and held together by every joint with which it is equipped, when each part is working properly, makes the body grow so that it builds itself up in love.
—Ephesians 4:15–16

Thomas asked Torrey to open in prayer, and when he was done, Thomas said, "It's been two weeks since our team-building retreat. How is everyone feeling about these two projects?"

Barry spoke first. "The people in our homeschool group seemed a little puzzled at first since we currently don't have any visible conflict with educational issues in our church. However, the idea of learning from one another to avoid any future misunderstandings seemed to find solid support."

Brent spoke next. "Overall, our public school parents showed no hesitation about joining the process. In fact, they have already

selected one couple to represent our group in any future panel discussions when that gets scheduled."

"Jenny, how is the scheduling coming?" Thomas asked.

"Over the next three months, we are planning to have all the
parent group meetings scheduled and have the panel discussion
ready too," Jenny replied. "Some of these meetings have already happened—like Barry's and Brent's groups—and we hope to have all
the panel discussion participants selected in the next several weeks."

"Great work, Jenny. Keep me posted on your progress."

Thomas then advised them to watch for any signs of misunderstandings or friction—either between individuals or
groups—during this process so they can offer assistance if needed.
"Anything else before we move on to our mediation training process?" Thomas asked, looking around. "Okay, if not, let's talk about
our training project."

Thomas looked at Danika and Torrey and asked, "Can we begin
to construct a general outline of content for our conflict resolution
class?"

Torrey and Danika both began answering at the same time,
but Torrey signaled for Danika to go ahead.

"The video series I mentioned provided some good ideas for our
course, and Torrey and I worked together to come up with a list of
suggested topics. We can also include additional scriptural references
and illustrations to show biblical connections and principles so our
church can see clear spiritual principles for this training," Danika said.

Torrey took it from there. "Mediation, as we've discussed, is a
biblical practice firmly rooted in Scripture. Matthew 18 provides a
basic outline. Most people engage in mediation at some level, even
if only in very informal settings like family disputes." He added that
mediation practice could run all the way from informally assisting
others in dispute resolution to formal court-based mediations.

Torrey shared two other resources, both mediation training

manuals, one from a secular training organization[45] and the other from a Christian conciliation ministry.[46] He said, "From these I believe we should be able to create a training process that is biblical and is also aligned with best practice guidelines. I've created a matrix with a sample schedule and content suggestions for the thirteen-week class as a starting point," he added and showed a slide for the staff members to review.

WEEK	TOPICS	DESCRIPTION
Week 1	Introduction to Christian mediation	Theology and overview of the Christian mediation process
Weeks 2–4	Mediation process and communication skills	Understanding of mediation steps and skill-building in communication strategies and techniques
Weeks 5–7	Conflict analysis and mediation role-play	Understanding the levels of conflict and practicing communication and mediation skills using case studies
Weeks 8–10	Working with groups	Understanding the facilitated problem-solving process
Weeks 11–13	Group problem-solving role-plays	Practice of facilitated problem-solving skills using case studies

"Thanks, Torrey and Danika; this is a great start!" Brent said.

"I enjoy helping people in conflict, and I've included everything Danika and I could think of that has helped us over the years," Torrey responded.

"We really do appreciate this good work," Thomas added. "Now perhaps you can help us understand what we are looking at!"

"Sure." Torrey explained that the course schedule included theological and theoretical components as well as opportunities for practice and role-play sessions, and he asked the group to look at the descriptions of terms.[47]

Mediation Course Terminology

1. **Negotiation:** A collaborative bargaining relationship between parties who have a perceived or actual conflict of interest.

2. **Mediation:** A facilitated negotiation process that involves the intervention of an acceptable third party who has limited (or no) authoritative decision-making power.

3. **Multiparty Mediation:** Mediations that involve more than two people (mediations with more than five parties will be considered group facilitation).

4. **Facilitated Problem-Solving:** Working with groups to improve their effectiveness in resolving problems collaboratively.

5. **Arbitration:** Arbitration is a generic term for a voluntary process in which people in conflict request the assistance of an impartial and neutral third party (or panel) to make a decision for them regarding contested issues.

6. **Levels of Conflict:** Refers to "locations" or "domains" of conflict including intrapersonal, interpersonal, intragroup, intergroup, and structural levels.

7. **Opening Statements:** Introductory comments made by the mediator to prepare the parties for the mediation process.

8. **Ground Rules:** Behavioral guidelines usually decided on jointly to help provide civil and collaborative structure to the mediation process.

9. **Caucus:** A brief recess during a mediation in which one or both parties meet privately with the mediator to discuss issues, concerns, questions, and/or strategies.

10. **Positions:** A stance taken based on the party's perceived needs.

11. **Interests:** The needs, desires, hopes, and fears leading parties to take a certain position.

12. **Framing:** The party's conceptualization of a conflict or situation.

13. **Reframing:** Changing the conceptualization of a conflict or situation to make it easier to conduct collaborative problem-solving.

14. **Agreement to Mediate:** Pre-mediation form signed by both parties indicating their good-faith intentions to participate in a mediation.

15. **Settlement Agreement:** Written agreement form signed by both parties indicating their acceptance of the stipulations in their mediated settlement.

Thomas suggested that Torrey go through the definitions to help the group get a feel for how the content of the course and the role-plays would tie together.

"Let's look at this curriculum a few weeks at a time," Torrey suggested, and he took the group through the plan.

> **Week One**: In the first week, we will consider an overview of Mediation and Christian Conciliation practices to see how the secular model aligns well with the biblical one. We will also learn about the Dispute Resolution Continuum. The terms *negotiation, mediation,* and *arbitration* closely parallel the Matthew 18 model, with negotiation equating to the first step: two people seeking to resolve their issues between themselves. Mediation parallels with the second step: inviting a third party to assist in the discussion, and the arbitration model is closely aligned with Matthew's third step: taking the matter to the church for a final determination.

> **Weeks Two through Four**: At the beginning of each class, we will do a quick review and answer any questions from our previous session. We'll watch a video of an actual mediation, so we can see how the process naturally unfolds. We'll focus on improving our communication skills with both instruction and a video illustrating healthy communication techniques. These skills will be correlated to biblical passages teaching the principles supporting these techniques. And lastly, we'll use role-play scenarios to practice what we have learned.

Weeks Five through Seven: Beginning on week five, we'll focus on conflict analysis using the Levels of Conflict diagram—to learn how we can better sort out the types of conflict in a dispute and frame an intervention strategy appropriate for the different levels. We'll then focus on the dynamics and intervention needed for interpersonal conflict, since this is where almost all conflicts surface regardless of which level the root causes can be found. We will study how Scripture can be used effectively in conflict resolution and provide a list of passages most helpful in the mediation process. We will discuss how to create a positive environment for the mediation through the use of opening statements by the mediator and then practice these skills in role-plays using case studies and debriefing to share insights.

Weeks Eight through Ten: In our next classes, we once again review and have a Q&A session to (a) make sure everyone is on the same page, and (b) clear up any confusion or unanswered questions from the previous sessions. This also serves as a review for anyone who missed a session. Then we will use both instruction and role-play exercises to learn and practice problem-solving facilitation.

Weeks Eleven through Thirteen: During our last three class periods, we look at special topics such as planning for follow-up with the parties after the mediation. And then we'll do more role-plays to practice the group facilitation skills that we've learned.

Torrey had concluded the summary and then asked, "So, what do you think?"

"It looks great to me!" Danika said, pleased.

"I think so too," Jenny added.

Thomas looked around the room, and everyone seemed to feel the same way. "Thanks again, Danika and Torrey," Thomas said. "Jenny, can you see when we can get this thirteen-session course on the church calendar?" he asked.

"Sure," she quickly replied.

Pastor Barrington and his staff were able to work together over the course of the next year, not only to successfully create a curriculum but also to train the pastoral staff in conflict intervention skills and to conduct numerous problem-solving sessions and mediations with several groups on a number of difficult issues.

The panel on school choices was also a great success. Not everyone agreed in the end, but those who disagreed were able to see other points of view and better understand and accept the differing decisions of other families in the church. And by the end of the year, a second Healthy Community Team at Riverdale Church had been trained,[48] and all indicators were that the church as a whole was beginning to recognize the value of this important new ministry.

Conclusion

A Job Well Done

All this is from God, who through Christ reconciled
us to himself and gave us the ministry of reconciliation.
—2 Corinthians 5:18

His master said to him, "Well done, good and faithful servant."
—Matthew 25:21

We began this journey with the story of Calvary Community Church. Things did not look good for this small congregation as Pastor Greg and his district superintendent discussed the congregation's decline into an ugly and prolonged church battle. But God did a miraculous work in the hearts of those leaders and church members. They did not sit idly by and allow their church to disintegrate. They prayed. They enthusiastically engaged the conflict in healthy ways using biblical principles, and they redeemed difficult circumstances for good. By God's grace and the diligent work of these leaders, Calvary Community Church is a healthy and thriving congregation today. But there is one telling experience not yet shared about this church.

Near the end of Calvary's conflict resolution process, the district superintendent was invited back to speak to the congregation in a public celebration service. Here is his account of that day:

On a Sunday we were there to celebrate the two-year journey we had just completed. I was sitting in the second or third row on the right-hand side. I greeted a man who sat down in a seat behind me. He told me that he was from out of town and that it was his first time visiting the church. In fact, he said that he wasn't a regular churchgoer. He was attending because of some family connection, although he was there alone that day. Since I knew our topic of the day was conflict in the church, I was concerned about what kind of impression the service might make on a first-time visitor, so I cautioned him that this wasn't going to be a typical service. Once the service was over, I spoke with him again. He gushed, "This was the most wonderful church service I've ever been to in my life!" Far from being put off by the acknowledgment of conflict in the church, he was amazed and attracted by the way the church had worked through their conflict until they restored right relationships.[49]

God is calling each of us to be faithful in the ministry of reconciliation. If this is true for all believers, how much more so for those leading and setting examples before congregations. Conflicts in the church are inevitable. They can either bring dishonor to the Lord or they can provide transformational opportunities like the one at Calvary Church.

The process presented in this book provides a road map to help church leaders recognize the dangers and create a clear pathway to restore broken relationships and create healthy community in their congregations. As the stories in this book reflect, conflicts and churches can be very different. But the biblical principles to address and resolve these disputes are the same.

When to call for outside assistance

It is wonderful when church leaders themselves can successfully resolve individual and systemic conflicts within their churches. This should be a normal part of church life and ministry. However, sometimes something more is needed. Matthew 18:15–17 describes the best first step to resolve interpersonal conflict—in the smallest circle possible. With personal conflict, this happens as two people meet together privately to seek good solutions— and in most cases the conflict doesn't need to go beyond those two participants. But when resolution is not achieved, the next step is to bring in someone else to help.

In a similar way, when a congregation attempts to resolve issues internally and then finds that they are unable to achieve a healthy resolution, it may be time to seek outside assistance. This can be true whether you need effective conflict resolution training or are looking to find a skillful interventionist.

Whether you use this road map to train your leaders and to intervene in the conflicts you encounter or you choose to invite others to help, it is my prayer that you and your church leaders find this book a helpful tool in better analyzing and resolving the conflicts and that you see God turn challenging circumstances into transformational opportunities for great blessing!

APPENDIXES

APPENDIX A

Chapter Exercise

PRESENTING ISSUE(S)	CONFLICT LEVEL(S)	RATIONALE
1. Les vs. Curtis 2. Youth Ministry vs. Parents 3. Staff vs. Board 4. Disagreement(s) within Board 5. Disagreement(s) among Parents 6. Other potential disagreements within Staff 7. Congregation vs. Staff 8. Congregation vs. Board 9. Potential disagreements within Congregation 10. Potential disagreements within Youth Group involving both Leaders and Youth	**Intrapersonal:** (not apparent yet; will manifest as process develops) **Interpersonal:** Les and Curtis (others will surface moving forward) **Intragroup:** Disagreements within the Staff, the Board, the Youth Group, Parents & Leaders & the Congregation **Intergroup:** Youth Ministry vs. Parents, Staff vs. Board, Congregation vs. Staff, Congregation vs. Board **Structural:** (will be revealed moving through the process)	—Recognizing where the conflict is surfacing is the starting place. We will be able to recognize underlying root causes as we move forward. —Les and Curtis's relationship is damaged. Other damaged relationships will emerge. —Factions often develop within ministry subgroups. —Ministry subgroups often find themselves on different sides of an issue. Leadership, organizational, policy, cultural deficits are revealed as process develops.

Healthy Community
Team Nominating Process

(Adapted and used with permission from
Living Stones Associates; documents by Eddy Hall)

Voting

1. Distribute Round 1 ballot. Do NOT explain what the purpose of this ballot is beyond the fact that this is to help select the members of the Healthy Community Team.

2. Distribute Round 2 ballot. Explain that on this ballot it is okay to duplicate names used on the first ballot. The important thing is to name those people who best represent these competencies, regardless of whether they were or were not named on the first ballot.

3. After collecting the second ballot, then explain that the first two ballots will be used to select the chair or co-chairs of the Healthy Community Team. Explain that the reason for two ballots is that most churches have a leadership selection culture that tends to focus primarily on either character or on competencies. However, both character and competencies are equally important for effective leadership in this position. Therefore, the Healthy Community Team chair will be selected from among those who receive a high number of votes on both ballots.

4. Distribute the Round 3 ballot. Explain that this ballot lists a combination of character qualities and competencies. This ballot is to nominate people for the remaining positions on the Healthy Community Team. *It is all right to duplicate names that they used on the first two ballots.*

5. Explain that you will rely heavily on these nominations in forming the Healthy Community Team (HCT), but make clear that this is a nominating ballot, not an electoral ballot. The HCT leadership team (and the pastor, if appropriate), guided by the nominating ballot, will invite one or two people to chair the team. Then the HCT leaders and the chair(s) (and the pastor, if appropriate) will together go through the remaining names nominated and will invite others to serve on the team. Explain that it is important that the leaders of the HCT have a strong say in who serves on those teams.

Selecting the team members

1. Tally the votes for each of the three ballots. If someone listed more than the number of names specified, pro-rate the votes. For example, if someone lists three names (rather than two) on Ballot 1, allocate each person two-thirds of a vote.

2. Identify one or more people who received a high number of votes on both of the first two ballots. If more than one person appears to be qualified, consider naming a chair and an assistant chair to the team. If the church is not involved in conflict to which the pastor is a party, discuss the top names with the pastor to determine if there is any reason that the top vote-getters might not be a suitable Healthy Community Team chair. If you have had previous opportunity to meet with these people, draw on your interaction with them in making your choice.

As you review names, keep in mind that this is a discernment process, not a popular election. The primary value of the balloting process is to determine which leaders in the church are most trusted.

3. Invite one or two leaders to chair the Healthy Community Team. If you invite two, first ask one to chair, then ask that person how he or she would feel about the other person serving as assistant chair. Go with the assistant chair only if the chair is

enthusiastic about the arrangement. Otherwise, go with just the single chair.

4. Meet with the chair(s) of the Healthy Community Team (and the pastor, if appropriate) to go over the remaining nominated names. Suggest the ground rule that anyone there can veto any name on the list for any reason or for no stated reason at all, if the person feels the person is not qualified to serve. The reason for allowing someone to be vetoed without stating a reason is so that people who have access to confidential information can veto on that basis without compromising a confidence.

Go through the names on the third ballot, beginning with those who have the most votes, discussing whether they would be good for the team. Cross-reference how many votes these names received on the first two ballots. It is probably good to not include on the team any people who received no votes on the first round (character qualities). Depending on the number of ballots, you might decide that no one should be included on the team if they received fewer than two votes on the first ballot.

An optimum size for a Healthy Community Team is seven people.

If you do not come up with enough names using this ballot process, brainstorm about people who may have been overlooked. For example, is there a spiritually mature high school student who may have been overlooked because of his or her age but who would bring a valuable perspective to the team?

5. Ask the Healthy Community Team chair to call each of those selected to invite them to serve.

6. Schedule the first meeting of the Healthy Community Team.

Healthy Community Team Ballot

Round 1 of nomination: Character qualities

Name one or two people, active in the life of this church, who you feel best exemplify the following character qualities:

Spiritually mature

Broadly respected

Respectful of differing viewpoints

Passionately committed to the mission of the church

Wise

Viewed as fair, even by most who disagree with them

Courageous: Willing to do what is right for the church, even in the face of criticism

_____

_____

Healthy Community Team Ballot

Round 2 of nomination: Competencies

Name one or two people who are an active part of the life of this congregation who you feel best exemplify the following competencies:

Collaborative: Good at helping to come up with win-win solutions

Team-builder: Has a track record of getting results through teams

Finisher: Has a track record of finishing what he or she starts

Creates safety: Has a track record of being able to create an environment in which people feel safe expressing their views and feelings, even though they know others in the group disagree with them.

_____

_____

Healthy Community Team Ballot

Round 3: Character/competencies of team members

Name three to five people, active in the life of this church, who you feel best exemplify the following character qualities and competencies:

> Passionately committed to the mission of the church
>
> Respectful of differing viewpoints. When people express differing viewpoints to this person, they feel heard
>
> Respected by people who hold differing viewpoints
>
> Able and willing to respectfully express own viewpoint
>
> Collaborative: Desiring to come up with win-win solutions
>
> Team player: Works well in groups to discuss, decide, and implement

_____

_____

APPENDIX C

Mediation Resources

https://www.mediate.com/index.cfm is a comprehensive source on the topic. Within this site, you will find mediation standards at https://www.mediate.com/articles/model_standards_of_conflict.cfm.

The American Bar Association provides information at: https://www.americanbar.org/groups/dispute_resolution/policy_standards/.

You may also view the webpage for the Association of Conflict Resolution: https://acrnet.org/page/ModelS.

Mediation standards are regulated at the state level. You may visit your own state government website for mediation standards for your jurisdiction. As an example, standards for the state of Colorado are found at: www.courts.state.co.us/userfiles/File/Administration/Executive/ODR/ADR_Professionals/Colorado_Model_Standards2000.doc.

You may also view more about mediation standards and get samples at: www.mediate.com/articles/melamed6.cfm.

Certification Course Matrix[50]

TIMES	WEEK ONE	WEEK TWO	WEEK THREE	WEEK FOUR	WEEK FIVE
8:00–10:00	Introduction to Mediation and Christian Conciliation	Review and Q&A/ Levels of Conflict and Conflict Analysis	Review and Q&A/ Defining the Issues and Setting the Agenda	Review and Q&A/ Multiparty Mediation	Review and Q&A/ Special Topics
9:00–10:00	Dispute Resolution Continuum	Interpersonal Conflict Dynamics	Positions and Interests	Setting the stage—room arrangement	Designing Agreements
10:00–10:15	Break	Break	Break	Break	Break
10:15–12:00	The Mediation Process & Video	Using Scripture in Mediation	Framing and Reframing	Facilitated Problem-Solving with Groups	Follow-up planning
12:00–12:30	Lunch	Lunch	Lunch	Lunch	Lunch
12:30–3:00	Communication Skills & Video	Opening Statements- Mediation Role-plays and Debriefs	Positions and Interests- Mediation Role-plays	Multiparty Mediation- Role-plays	Putting It All Together- Full Mediation- Role-plays and Debriefs
3:00–3:15	Break	Break	Break	Break	Break
3:15–5:00	Communication Role-plays and Debriefs	Creating a Positive Environment -Mediation Role-plays and Debriefs	Framing and Reframing - Mediation Role-plays and Debriefs	Facilitated Problem-Solving- Role-plays and Debriefs	Putting It All Together- Full Mediation- Role-plays and Debriefs

---

Sample Interview Questions

Below are some examples of open-ended, neutral questions that are useful in collecting data for the conflict resolution process analysis.

1. What are your most significant concerns related to past and current conflicts?

2. Have you personally contributed to these problems? Have you had opportunity to help resolve them?

3. In your opinion, who should be a part of any efforts to address these issues?

4. If you could imagine a dream solution in this situation, what would it look like?

(compressed here to save space)

Analyzing Data Gathered from Interviews

Once the information is gathered, identified issues can be categorized by conflict level. The matrix below can be used for the purpose of recording representative quotes. If the interviewee population is diverse enough to capture all or most of the existing groups/opinions/factions, patterns will become evident. Dominant themes usually emerge, indicating the most significant concerns among those interviewed, while at the same time, less significant issues usually become apparent by the infrequency or inconsistency of their occurrence.

INTRA-PERSONAL	INTER-PERSONAL	INTRAGROUP	INTERGROUP	STRUCTURAL

APPENDIX F

Conflict Assessment Tool

Levels of Conflict

1. Is the conflict between two or three individuals, or does it involve identified groups? (if both, answer B)

    A) Individuals

    B) Groups

2. Has there been only one conflict event, or have there been several similar or related conflicts?

    A) One event

    B) Multiple events

3. If multiple, are the same or different people involved in each conflict?

    A) Same individuals

    B) Different individuals

4. Are there any structural factors (financial, theological, political, organizational, cultural, etc.) that may be contributing to the conflict(s)?

    A) No

    B) Yes

Relational Dynamics

5. How have the parties responded to each other during these disagreements?

    A) Heated arguments

    B) Civil dialogue

6. Is there any indication that Matthew 18 principles are being followed?

    A) No

    B) Yes

7. How have church leaders responded to the conflict(s)?

    A) Avoidance

    B) Engagement

8. If engaged, are the leaders becoming divided over the conflict?

    A) Yes

    B) No

INTERPRETING YOUR ANSWERS

Levels of Conflict

Questions 1–4: If you answer A to all these questions, your conflict(s) may be limited in scope to the interpersonal level. If you answer B to any of these questions, root causes most likely extend to the structural level.

Relational Dynamics

Questions 6–8: If you answer A to all or most of these questions, it potentially reflects an unhealthy leadership culture. If you answer B to all or most of these questions, your leadership culture shows signs of good health.

Question 1—If a conflict involves only a few individuals, it is likely that the root cause can be found either within one or more individuals (intrapersonal level conflict) or between individuals (interpersonal level conflict). It is important to understand that conflict on these two levels requires different intervention strategies than when groups are involved (intragroup level conflict and/or intergroup level conflict).

Question 2—If there has been only a single conflict event, it is possible that it represents an isolated circumstance that requires only a limited intervention. If there are multiple conflict events, it is wise to look for commonalities (patterns) to provide insights into larger group or structural issues.

Question 3—If the same people are involved in multiple conflicts, it is possible that the conflict is limited in scope to these individuals (either intrapersonal or interpersonal level conflict). If different people are involved in similar types of conflict, it may point to group or structural root causes.

Question 4—This is a reminder to leaders to look more deeply into conflict episodes to see if structural issues are at play (financial, theological, political, organizational, cultural, etc.). These factors are the most significant and least visible contributors to conflict. Looking for patterns is one of the best ways to identify structural root causes.

Question 5—The way people (particularly leaders) respond to conflict is one of the most accurate predictors of whether the conflict will escalate or become well-managed and resolved.

Question 6—If Matthew 18 principles are being followed, it indicates above-average teaching and a healthy church culture regarding interpersonal conflict resolution. If not, it signals an invitation to leaders to bring focus on these principles. However, churches will likely experience repeated conflicts if the other levels of conflict are not recognized and addressed.

Question 7—See question 5. Unless leaders are practicing healthy conflict resolution responses and engagement, it is unlikely that the congregation will do any better. This question helps church leaders self-evaluate and take appropriate action.

Question 8—If leadership is divided, serious schism in the church is likely to follow.

Conflict Management Style Survey

In this section you will have the opportunity to examine your own conflict-management style and techniques that you tend to use in conflict situations, particularly under stress. The exercises that follow will enable you to gain insight into strategies you might choose to incorporate into your behavior in handling disputes and differences.

Conflict-Management Style Survey*

This Conflict-Management Style Survey has been designed to help you become more aware of your characteristic approach, or style, in managing conflict. In completing this survey, you are invited to respond by making choices that correspond with your typical behavior or attitudes in conflict situations.

Section 1: Survey

This survey identifies twelve situations that you are likely to encounter in your personal and professional lives. Please study each situation and the five possible behavioral responses or attitudes carefully and then allocate ten points between them to indicate your typical behavior, with the highest number of points indicating your strongest choice. Any response can be answered with from zero to ten points, as long as all five responses for a given situation add up to ten points, as shown in the following example:

EXAMPLE SITUATION: In responding to a request from another for help with a problem, you would:

4 A. Clearly instruct him or her how to proceed.

2 B. Enjoy the strategizing and the challenge.

3 C. Help him or her take responsibility for the problem.

1 D. Find it unnerving but agree to help.

0 E. Avoid the invitation at all costs.

10 TOTAL

Please choose a single frame of reference (e.g., work-related conflicts, family conflicts, social conflicts) and keep that frame of
reference in mind when responding to all the situations. And remember, as you complete this survey, that it is not a test. There
are no right or wrong responses. The survey will be helpful to you
only to the extent that your responses accurately represent your
characteristic behavior or attitudes.

SITUATION 1: Upon experiencing strong feelings in a conflict situation, you would:

A. Enjoy the emotional release and sense of exhilaration and
accomplishment.

B. Enjoy the strategizing involved and the challenge of the
conflict.

C. Become serious about how others are feeling and thinking.

D. Find it frightening because you do not accept that differences can be discussed without someone getting hurt.

E. Become convinced that there is nothing you can do to
resolve the issue.

TOTAL

*Based on Jay Hall's *Conflict Management Survey: A Survey of One's
Characteristic Reaction to and Handling of Conflict Between Himself
and Others* (The Woodlands, TX: Telemetrics International, 1969).

SITUATION 2: Consider the following statements and rate them in terms of how characteristic they are of your personal beliefs:

    A. Life is conquered by those who believe in winning.

    B. Winning is rarely possible in conflict.

    C. No one has the final answer to anything, but each has a piece to contribute.

    D. In the last analysis, it is wise to turn the other cheek.

    E. It is useless to attempt to change a person who seems locked into an opposing view.

    TOTAL

SITUATION 3: What is the best result that you expect from conflict?

    A. Conflict helps people face the fact that one answer is better than others.

    B. Conflict results in canceling out extremes of thinking so that a strong middle ground can be reached.

    C. Conflict clears the air and enhances commitment and results.

    D. Conflict demonstrates the absurdity of self-centeredness and draws people closer together in their commitment to each other.

    E. Conflict lessens complacency and assigns blame where it belongs.

    TOTAL

SITUATION 4: When you are the person with the greater authority in a conflict situation, you would:

    A. Put it straight, letting the other know your view.

    B. Try to negotiate the best settlement you can get.

C. Ask to hear the other's feelings and suggest that a position be found that both might be willing to try.

D. Go along with the other, providing support where you can.

E. Keep the encounter impersonal, citing rules if they apply.

TOTAL

SITUATION 5: When someone you care for takes an unreasonable position, you would:

A. Lay it on the line, telling him or her that you don't like it.

B. Let him or her know in casual, subtle ways that you are not pleased; possibly distract with humor; and avoid a direct confrontation.

C. Call attention to the conflict and explore a mutually acceptable solution.

D. Try to keep your misgivings to yourself.

E. Let your actions speak for you by indicating depression or lack of interest.

TOTAL

SITUATION 6: When you become angry at a friend or colleague, you would:

A. Just explode without giving it much thought.

B. Try to smooth things over with a good story.

C. Express your anger and invite him or her to respond.

D. Try to compensate for your anger by acting the opposite of what you are feeling.

E. Remove yourself from the situation.

TOTAL

SITUATION 7: When you find yourself disagreeing with other members of a group on an important issue, you would:

    A. Stand by your convictions and defend your position.

    B. Appeal to the logic of the group in the hope of convincing at least a majority that you are right.

    C. Explore points of agreement and disagreement and the feelings of the group's members, and then search for alternatives that take everyone's views into account.

    D. Go along with the rest of the group.

    E. Not participate in the discussion and not feel bound by any decision reached.

    TOTAL

SITUATION 8: When a single group member takes a position in opposition to the rest of the group, you would:

    A. Point out publicly that the dissenting member is blocking the group and suggest that the group move on without him or her if necessary.

    B. Make sure the dissenting member has a chance to communicate his or her objections so that a compromise can be reached.

    C. Try to uncover why the dissenting member views the issue differently, so that the group's members can reevaluate their own positions.

    D. Encourage the group's members to set the conflict aside and go on to more agreeable items on the agenda.

    E. Remain silent, because it is best to avoid becoming involved.

    TOTAL

SITUATION 9: When you see conflict emerging in a group, you would:

    A. Push for a quick decision to ensure that the task is completed.

    B. Avoid outright confrontation by moving the discussion toward a middle ground.

    C. Share with the group your impression of what is going on, so that the nature of the impending conflict can be discussed.

    D. Forestall or divert the conflict before it emerges by relieving the tension with humor.

    E. Stay out of the conflict as long as it is of no concern to you.

    TOTAL

SITUATION 10: In handling conflict between your group and another, you would:

    A. Anticipate areas of resistance and prepare responses to objections prior to open conflict.

    B. Encourage your group's members to be prepared by identifying in advance areas of possible compromise.

    C. Recognize that conflict is healthy and press for the identification of shared concerns and/or goals.

    D. Promote harmony on the grounds that the only real result of conflict is the destruction of friendly relations.

    E. Have your group submit the issue to an impartial arbitrator.

    TOTAL

SITUATION 11: In selecting a member of your group to represent you in negotiating with another group, you would choose a person who:

   A. Knows the rationale of your group's position and would press vigorously for your group's point of view.

   B. Would see that most of your group's judgments were incorporated into the final negotiated decision without alienating too many members of either group.

   C. Would best represent the ideas of your group, evaluate these in view of judgments of the other group, and then emphasize problem-solving approaches to the conflict.

   D. Is most skillful in interpersonal relations and would be openly cooperative and tentative in his or her approach.

   E. Would present your group's case accurately, while not making commitments that might result in obligating your group to a significantly changed position.

   TOTAL

SITUATION 12: In your view, what might be the reason for the failure of one group to collaborate with another?

   A. Lack of a clearly stated position, or failure to back up the group's position.

   B. Tendency of groups to force their leadership or representatives to abide by the group's decision, as opposed to promoting flexibility, which would facilitate compromise.

   C. Tendency of groups to enter negotiations with a win/lose perspective.

   D. Lack of motivation on the part of the group's membership to live peacefully with the other group.

    E. Irresponsible behavior on the part of the group's leadership, resulting in the leaders placing emphasis on maintaining their own power positions rather than addressing the issues involved.

TOTAL

Section 2: Scoring

Step 1

When you have completed all items in Section 1, write the number of points you assigned for each of the five responses for the twelve situations in the appropriate columns on the scoring form (figure 26). Add the total number of points for each column, then check that the totals for each column add up to 120.

Step 2

Transfer your column total scores onto the form showing the ideal order (figure 27).

Step 3

Transfer the style names, in order of the highest score first, onto figure 28, which shows your order, and then enter the scores in the adjacent blank spaces.

Step 4

Record your scores in the appropriate blanks on the Conflict-Management Styles Scoring Graph (figure 29). (You may wish to refresh your memory by reviewing the material describing the five conflict styles presented in chapter 11.)

SITUATION	RESPONSE A	RESPONSE B	RESPONSE C	RESPONSE D	RESPONSE E	TOTAL
1						10
2						10
3						10
4						10
5						10
6						10
7						10
8						10
9						10
10						10
11						10
12						10
TOTAL						120

Figure 26. Scoring form.

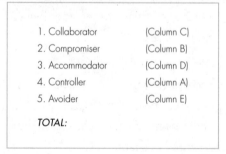

1. Collaborator   (Column C)
2. Compromiser   (Column B)
3. Accommodator   (Column D)
4. Controller   (Column A)
5. Avoider   (Column E)

TOTAL:

Figure 27

Choice	Style	Score
1st	_____	_____
2nd	_____	_____
3rd	_____	_____
4th	_____	_____
5th	_____	_____

TOTAL:

Figure 28. Your order.

Competing/Controlling is assertive and uncooperative—an individual pursues his or her own concerns at the other person's expense. This is a power-oriented mode, in which one uses whatever power seems appropriate to win one's own position—one's ability to argue, one's rank, or economic sanctions. Competing might mean "standing up for one's rights," defending a position which you believe is correct, or simply trying to win.

Accommodating is unassertive and cooperative—the opposite of competing. When accommodating, an individual neglects his or her own concerns to satisfy the concerns of the other person; there is an element of self-sacrifice in this mode.

Accommodating might take the form of selfless generosity or charity, obeying another person's order when one would prefer not to, or yielding to another's point of view.

Avoiding is unassertive and uncooperative—the individual does not immediately pursue his own concerns or those of the other person. He or she does not address the conflict. Avoiding might take the form of diplomatically sidestepping an issue, postponing an issue until a better time, or simply withdrawing from a threatening situation.

Collaborating is both assertive and cooperative—the opposite of avoiding. Collaborating involves an attempt to work with the other person to find some solution that fully satisfies the concerns of both persons. It means digging into an issue to identify the underlying concerns of the two individuals and to find an alternative that meets both sets of concerns. Collaborating between two persons might take the form of exploring a disagreement to learn from each other's insights, concluding to resolve some condition that would otherwise have them competing for resources or confronting and trying to find a creative solution to an interpersonal problem.

Compromising is intermediate in both assertiveness and cooperativeness. The object is to find some expedient, mutually acceptable solution that partially satisfies both parties. It falls on a middle ground between competing and accommodating. Compromising gives up more than competing but less than accommodating. Likewise, it addresses an issue more directly than avoiding but doesn't explore it in as much depth as collaborating. Compromising might mean splitting the difference, exchanging concessions, or seeking a quick middle-ground position.

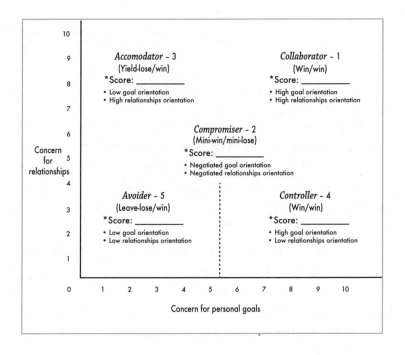

About the Author

Dr. Michael Hare has served over two decades in the role of senior pastor, primarily in church turnaround ministries; fifteen years working as a church conflict consultant; and most recently as staff chaplain and ombudsman at Compassion International. These opportunities have included:

- Leading turnaround interventions while pastoring diverse congregations from rural New England to middle-class suburbia to an inner city in Southern California.
- Serving as a church health consultant with successful interventions in more than thirty churches in a wide variety of denominations.
- Leading, training, and helping resolve cross-cultural conflicts involving multinational staff globally.

Dr. Hare holds a PhD in Conflict Analysis and Resolution and has also served as an adjunct instructor for several universities and colleges and is most recently teaching mediation courses in a doctoral program in Colorado. Michael and his wife, Colleen, live in Colorado Springs and have four children and six grandchildren who live in Africa and the U.S.

NOTES

1. Jim Van Yperen, *Making Peace: A Guide to Overcoming Church Conflict* (Chicago: Moody, 2008), 13.

2. David Van Biema, "Religion: Missionaries Under Cover," *Time*, June 30, 2003, https://web.archive.org/web/20070428234833/http://www.time.com/time/covers/1101030630/map. The link is to the map, which is part of an extensive cover story. The 10/40 Window is the area of North Africa, the Middle East and Asia approximately between 10 degrees north and 40 degrees north latitude. It has been called the "Resistant Belt" because it includes a majority of the world's Muslims, Hindus, and Buddhists.

3. *Healthy Community Team* refers to a small group of laypeople, carefully selected from the congregation based on their moral character and spiritual gifts, to help implement church health recommendations. See Appendix B.

4. Jay Rothman, *Resolving Identity-Based Conflict in Nations, Organizations, and Communities* (San Francisco: Jossey-Bass, 1997), 13.

5. Speed Leas, "How Bad Is the Conflict?" *Christianity Today*, January 1, 1989, https://www.christianitytoday.com/pastors/1989/winter/89l1016.html.

6. Don Hellriegel, John W. Slocum Jr., and Richard W. Woodman, *Organizational Behavior*, 5th ed. (St. Paul, MN: West Publishing Company, 1989).

7. Adapted from Dr. Michael Hare, "Conflict and Vision," *Outcomes*, Summer 2018, https://outcomesmagazine.com/conflict-and-vision.

8. Frederick F. Bruce, *New International Commentary on the New Testament: The Book of Acts* (Grand Rapids, MI: Eerdmans, 1979), 127.

9. Wallie A. Criswell, *Acts: An Exposition*, vol. 1 (Grand Rapids, MI: Zondervan, 1978), 202.

10. Eddy Hall, "Your Church's Conflict: God's Opportunity," Living Stones Associates, www.living-stones.com/church-conflict-consultation.html.

11. Gordon Marshall, *Oxford Dictionary of Sociology*, 2nd ed. (New York: Oxford University Press, 1998), s.v. "culture," 137.

12. Morgan Lee, "A Deeper Debate over Drums in Church: Native Christians Still Wrestle with How Their Culture Fits into Their Churches," *Christianity Today*, August 18, 2017, https://www.christianitytoday.com/ct/topics/w/worship-wars.

13. Máire Dugan, "A Nested Theory of Conflict," *A Leadership Journal: Women in Leadership—Sharing the Vision* 1, no. 1 (July 1996): 9–20, https://emu.edu/cms-links/cjp/docs/Dugan_Maire_Nested-Model-Original.pdf

14. Depending on organizational structure, policies, relational dynamics, and so on, the third party should be explicitly trusted by both parties and would normally correspond to the official reporting structure within the organization. If for some reason there is a trusted third party outside the reporting structure, this can work as long as it doesn't violate policy or bypass the accountability system.

15. Dallas Willard, *Renovation of the Heart: Putting on the Character of Christ* (Colorado Springs: NavPress, 2012), 19.

16. John MacArthur, *Matthew 16–23*, MacArthur New Testament Commentary (Chicago: Moody, 1988), 134–35.

17. For a detailed treatment of this subject, see Christopher W. Moore, *The Mediation Process: Practical Strategies for Resolving Conflict*, 4th ed. (San Francisco: John Wiley & Sons, 2014), 307–24.

18. For a list of mediation term definitions, see page 204 of this book.

19. Regulations regarding confidentiality in mediation can vary widely from state to state. Local laws should be researched and explained clearly to the parties early in the mediation process.

20. Bernard S. Mayer, *The Dynamics of Conflict Resolution: A Practitioner's Guide* (San Francisco: Jossey-Bass, 2000), 113.

21. MacArthur, *Matthew 16–23*, 145.

22. Some Bible teachers hold to the fact that we cannot forgive a person if they do not first repent. Others believe that reconciliation requires repentance but forgiveness does not. This author believes God's forgiveness is complete in Christ. Whether one receives it or not is up to us. Forgiving others as Christ has forgiven us is to forgive unconditionally, regardless of whether it is received or rejected.

23. Ken Sande, *The Peacemaker: A Biblical Guide to Resolving Personal Conflict* (Grand Rapids, MI: Baker, 2004).

24. Chelsea L. Greer and Everett L. Worthington Jr., *Experiencing Forgiveness: Six Practical Sessions for Becoming a More Forgiving Christian: Self-Directed Learning Workbook* (Richmond, VA: Virginia Commonwealth University), www.evworthington-forgiveness.com/diy-workbooks.

25. Kerry Patterson et al, *Crucial Conversations: Tools for Talking When Stakes Are High* (New York: McGraw Hill, 2012), 165.

26. Gary Chapman and Jennifer Thomas, *When Sorry Isn't Enough: Making Things Right with Those You Love* (Chicago: Northfield, 2013).

27. R. H. Kilmann and K. W. Thomas. http://www.kilmanndiagnostics.com/overview-thomas-kilmann-conflict-mode-instrument-tki. For a sample assessment using this approach, see Appendix G.

28. Eddy Hall, used with permission.

29. Don Fortune and Katie Fortune, *Discover Your God-Given Gifts* (Grand Rapids, MI: Chosen Books, 2009).

30. Ken Sande, "Six Relational Disciplines," Relational Wisdom 360, https://rw360.org.

31. Travis Bradberry and Jean Greaves, *Emotional Intelligence 2.0* (San Diego: Talent Smart, 2009).

32. Peacemaker Ministries, https://peacemaker.training/.

33. "Links to Resources for Those Interested in Education and Training from Christian Perspectives: Training in Peace and Conflict Work," Peacemakers Trust, www.peacemakers.ca/education/educationchristianlinks.html.

34. D. Edmond Hiebert, *The Epistle of James: Tests of a Living Faith* (Chicago: Moody, 1979), 73.

35. This refers to a biblical perspective of conflict in the context of God's designs and purposes for believers and for the church.

36. Adapted from Roger Schwarz, *The Skilled Facilitator: A Comprehensive Resource for Consultants, Facilitators, Managers, Trainers, and Coaches*, rev. ed. (San Francisco: Jossey-Bass, 2002) in *The IAF Handbook of Group Facilitation*, Sandy Schuman, ed. (San Francisco: Jossey-Bass, 2005), 22.

37. These ground rules and agenda ideas are adapted from Roger Schwarz, Anne Davidson, Peg Carlson, and Sue McKinney, *The Skilled Facilitator Fieldbook: Tips, Tools, and Tested Methods for Consultants, Facilitators, Managers, Trainers, and Coaches* (San Francisco: Jossey-Bass, 2009).

38. Eddy Hall, "When Conflict Interrupts Ministry," HeartWork for Christian Leaders, June 4, 2018, http://heartworkforleaders.living-stones.com/when-conflict-interrupts-ministry.

39. Roger Schwarz et al., *The Skilled Facilitator Fieldbook: Tips, Tools, and Tested Methods for Consultants, Facilitators, Managers, Trainers, and Coaches* (San Francisco: Jossey-Bass, 2009), 6.

40. John P. Kotter, *Leading Change* (Boston: Harvard Business Review Press, 2012).

41. Training sessions and interventions can also be arranged with outside ministries such as Living Stones Associates. For those desiring to create a more in-depth curriculum for the certification of mediators, see Appendix D.

42. Adapted from Living Stones Associates "Church Health Team Charter Template" created by Eddy Hall.

43. Some churches prefer a nomination process in identifying candidates for teams. One procedure for combining both character and competency qualities can be found in Appendix B.

44. "Resolving Everyday Conflict: Biblical Answers for a Common Problem" by Peacemaker Ministries is one resource suitable for providing a general overview of biblical conflict resolution and is available at www.rightnowmedia.org/Content/Series/157.

45. Retrieved from http://web.archive.org/web/20180127235734/http://www.campus-adr.org:80/cr_services_cntr/mit_all.pdf. (See also https://ceai.org.)

46. The Center for Conflict Resolution, www.ccr4peace.org/ccrhandbookbound.doc.

47. Some definitions adapted from Christopher W. Moore, *The Mediation Process: Practical Strategies for Resolving Conflict* (San Francisco: Jossey-Bass, 2014).

48. The number of teams needed will vary by congregation size and culture.

49. Used with permission.

50. Curriculum standards vary by state. Certified instructors are usually required to facilitate courses.

Acknowledgments

Loving thanks to my wife, Colleen, without whose encouragement and support this book could never have been possible.

I also wish to thank Sean Byrne, Brian Polkinghorn, Marcia Sweedler, and Judith McKay whose insights and inspiration in the study of conflict resolution have been instrumental in both theoretical and practical ways. My deep appreciation to Eddy Hall for his friendship and partnership in church consulting and for his willingness and time to review and offer editorial recommendations for each chapter.

A special word of thanks to the many pastors, church leaders, and church members who offered their collaborative insights during countless hours of interviews, mediations, and workshops and through which this content could be made practical.

Lastly and most importantly, I thank God for His loving grace in providing me the health and strength to take advantage of this opportunity for research and writing. I trust that He will be glorified in any contribution these pages offer to those leaders struggling to find help with resolving conflict in their time of need.

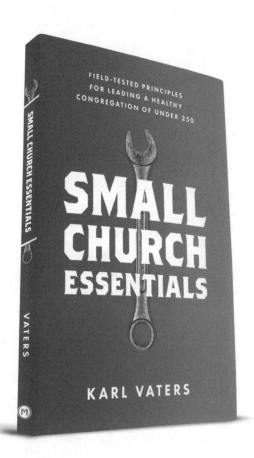

CAN WE ALL JUST GET ALONG?

J. BRIAN TUCKER & JOHN KOESSLER

ALL TOGETHER DIFFERENT

UPHOLDING THE CHURCH'S UNITY
WHILE HONORING OUR INDIVIDUAL IDENTITIES

TIMELESS TRUTH FROM J. OSWALD SANDERS

Sanders presents and illustrates several magnifying principles through the lives of prolific men. *Spiritual Leadership* will encourage you to place your talents and powers at God's disposal so you can become a leader used for His glory.

978-0-8024-1670-4

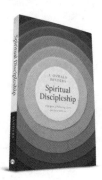

True discipleship is more than intellectual assent to a belief in Christ; it involves the whole person and lifestyle. This book will help you embody that truth. It examines Jesus' teaching on what it means to follow Him, helping you become the kind of Christian Jesus wants you to be—not one devised by man or even other Christians.

978-0-8024-1669-8

Spiritual maturity is not a level of growth Christians achieve, but the passion to press on in Christ. In this book, J. Oswald Sanders provides clear direction for those desiring to grow strong spiritually. Complete with scriptural principles for spiritual development and study questions at the end of the text, this classic handbook is a timeless treasure.

978-0-8024-1671-1

MOODY
Publishers®

From the Word to Life®

also available as eBooks